BRINGING UP BOYS

Tim Kahn

Piccadilly Press • London

*To my father, who taught me more about being a man
than I ever realised*

Typeset from author's disc by Piccadilly Press
Printed and bound by Creative Print and Design Wales
Piccadilly Press Ltd, 5 Castle Road, London NW1 8PR

A catalogue record for this book is available from
the British Library

ISBN: 1 85340 526 4

5 7 9 10 8 6 4

Other books in the How To Help Your Child series:
CHILD SAFETY FOR PARENTS
COMMUNICATING WITH YOUR TEENAGER
COPING WITH LOSS
GRAMMAR FOR PARENTS
INFORMATION TECHNOLOGY FOR PARENTS
MATHS FOR PARENTS
OVERCOME BULLYING FOR PARENTS
PRE-SCHOOL LEARNING FOR PARENTS
READING FOR PARENTS
SPELLING FOR PARENTS
WRITING FOR PARENTS

Cover design by Mandy Sherliker
Cover photograph © Katie Vandyck, 1998

ACKNOWLEDGEMENTS

In particular I would like to thank Margaret Gault and David Reid, who read and commented on early drafts and offered new perspectives on various topics. Thanks are also due to the many other friends, colleagues and parents who talked with me about bringing up boys over the recent months and years and, of course, my family for allowing me to 'practise' on them.

Tim Kahn is a father of two children, Ben and Sarah, aged eleven and thirteen. He has shared equally in the care of their upbringing with his wife. Since Ben was born Tim has been working in the field of parenting education and support, running groups for parents and writing about parenting issues. He has worked with many of the major national parenting and child welfare organisations, written for national newspapers and magazines, and worked with radio and television. He has a particular interest in fathers and sons.

CONTENTS

FOREWORD

You have probably bought this book because you want to understand more about bringing up boys. Perhaps you are finding it hard to deal with your sons' behaviour. Maybe you are a mother who finds your sons all the more incomprehensible – particularly if you did not grow up with any brothers – because they behave so differently from how you behaved when you were young. Maybe you are a father with a memory of your father taking a back seat in your upbringing who wants some ideas to help find a way to become more 'present' with your sons.

This book aims to identify those issues and difficulties that may exist because you have a son (as opposed to a daughter) – and which aren't just individual difficulties that beset you and your particular family. The book is written with the idea of helping you understand why boys behave they way they do and the ways in which you can respond to them. There are, of course, no magic solutions but there are a range of practical tips that can make a world of difference.

INTRODUCTION

HISTORICAL CONTEXT

Boys and men have been centre-stage for thousands of years. What every father wanted was a son to be his heir, to follow in his footsteps. In fact, he often wanted a son in preference to a daughter.

A man was supposed to be strong and tough, and his role was to support his family. A woman was likely to look after the home; she might work from home to bring in extra income or otherwise acquire elegant accomplishments, depending on her class.

Changes in the relationship between men and women have been comparatively recent, so it is not surprising that traditional ways of thinking still abound. Rapid change happened in this century: after the First World War, women were finally enfranchised politically and they got the vote; during the Second World War, because the men had gone off to fight, large numbers of women had to go out to work and nurseries were provided to look after their children – though women mostly had to return home when the men came back from the war. Pressure for change from women continued until in the 1960s the women's movement started to demand equality for women in many spheres: women wanted control of their own lives, including financial independence from men; they wanted to break into the world of work and be able to pursue careers; and they wanted men to take on their fair share of the housework and child-rearing.

While women were embracing and struggling with these changes, what was happening to men? Men were to a large extent trying to carry on as if nothing had changed. Their traditional role gave them economic and political power, and they saw no advantage in giving this up.

Although women started to enter the world of work in ever-increasing numbers, men were not prepared to enter the world of the home and to take on a share of what was traditionally 'women's work'. If anything, they felt threatened by the advances that women were making and wanted to return to the world as they knew it. But the world of the two genders – the 'opposite' sexes, as they are called – could never be so opposite again.

HOME

As a direct result of these changes, many women reacted against the assumptions that lay behind the way they had been brought up. This influenced the way in which they related to their sons and daughters.

Mothers (and fathers) saw boys running around and playing with construction toys, while girls seemed to play quiet nurturing games with dolls. Boys immersed themselves in activity, primarily talking with others about what they were doing, while girls used play as a vehicle to talk about themselves and their feelings. Parents tried to influence what their children played with, but with limited success, as girls seemed to want to continue to play with their dolls while the only doll a boy would play with was Action Man, however much this was discouraged.

'I didn't like the way that I was brought up to do "girlie" things. I was certainly not going to bring Kirsty up like that. But I must say, the more I tried to wean her off her dolls and long frilly dresses, the more she wanted to play with her dolls and wear long frilly dresses. And it was similar with Jimmy: I couldn't get him away from boys' things either.

'A lot of my feminist friends had similar experiences. Our girls and boys did the things and played the games they wanted, rather than what we hoped they would play.' Sarah

SCHOOL

The 1960s also saw a radical overhaul of the education system, with the introduction of comprehensive and coeducational schools at secondary level. Comprehensive education held out the vision of a society moving towards greater equality of opportunity, so with coeducational schools the scene was set for initiatives to increase gender equality.

There was growing concern with girls' underachievement in schools. It was recognised that girls were doing better than boys in the early years of schooling because they matured earlier, but by the time young people took their national exams in secondary school, boys had caught up with and overtaken girls, particularly in the traditionally male subjects of maths and science. In the 1980s a conscious decision was made to do something about this. This included an increasing emphasis on verbal skills, which favoured girls, and a reduction in competitive testing, which had previously favoured boys. Such initiatives, plus the fact that traditional male employment was disappearing fast, have meant that girls' academic achievements have now surpassed boys' (see the statistics below).

If the concern in the 1980s was for girls, the concern today is for boys. Many boys seem to have responded to the growing evidence of girls' increasing academic achievement by opting out of education and messing around while they are in school. In the 1980s there was talk about educating girls separately from boys so that girls would be able to achieve their full potential and not be held back by boys. The tables have now turned, and a growing number of schools are reintroducing old-fashioned testing, combining this with less emphasis on verbal skills and even teaching boys separately in some subjects, as this seems to help boys overcome the new gender gap in achievement.

SOME STATISTICS

SCHOOL

The following statistics are taken from *Can boys do better?*, produced by the Secondary Heads Association (1997):

- girls outperform boys at GCSE in all but Double Science;
- twice as many girls get a grade A at GCSE English as boys;

- girls outperform boys at A level.

As recently as the 1980s it was boys who performed better in all these areas. Some of the reasons given for boys' failure to do so well are:

- they are twice as likely as girls not to do homework, to play truant and to miss lessons;
- a disproportionate number of boys cause problems in the classroom through disruptive and antisocial behaviour:
    - 80 per cent of pupils excluded from secondary schools and 92 per cent from primary schools are boys, and
    - boys outnumber girls by six to one in special units for pupils with behavioural difficulties.

Despite the evidence, boys still claim, in all honesty, that they are cleverer than girls! They say that they just *pretend* not to be clever, because girls like the boys who are not clever. This suggests that boys find it easier to opt out of, rather than face, the growing challenge from girls and the fear of failure and peer-group scorn.

THE WORLD OF WORK

The world of work, traditionally 'his domain', is changing beyond all recognition. More statistics from *Can boys do better?* show the following:

- it is estimated that by the year 2000 more women will be in employment than men;
- on existing trends, by the year 2000 there will be

300,000 fewer 'male' jobs and 500,000 more 'female' jobs;
• more of the new jobs that are being created are part-time as opposed to full-time; currently two-fifths of women work part-time, whereas only one-tenth of men do;
• in July 1998 38,000 males between the ages of 18 and 24 had been unemployed for over a year, but only 13,000 females (these figures from the Department for Education and Employment).

The man's role as sole or main breadwinner has all but disappeared. Traditionally, men gained their sense of identity from the work that they did, but now they need to find ways of developing a new, broader identity. However, they are finding it hard to change. Although women are rapidly taking their place in the job market, men are frequently reluctant to take on a larger share of the work at home. So in many ways boys are not seeing their fathers embracing new roles in the way that girls see their mothers do.

ROLES IN THE HOME
Despite the growing rejection of the idea of traditional roles for men and women, recent British Social Attitudes Surveys show that on balance the belief prevails that 'a husband's job is to earn the money [and] a wife's job is to look after home and family'. This may help to explain why in 75 per cent of households women are still 'mainly responsible for general domestic duties', despite the large increase in dual-earner households.

Similarly, the evidence suggests that women are responsible for much of the care of young children, with one survey showing that mothers put in a massive 87 per cent of the 50 or so hours a week involved.

So boys (and girls) are still likely to see their mothers doing the bulk of the housework and childcare in the 'modern family'.

Boys' Responses in a Changing World
Crime
Crime is a singularly male problem: over 80 per cent of known offenders are male. The disparity in the involvement of males and females in crime starts when they are young. Angela Phillips in *The Trouble with Boys* quotes the following statistics:

- boys are nearly 6 times as likely as girls to be cautioned or found guilty of indictable offences;
- 15- and 16-year-old boys are 60 times more likely to be imprisoned than girls of the same age.

When a boy feels that the system has failed him, he is much more likely than a girl to turn his anger against the world. In fact, hitting out against authority by turning to crime can be seen as a way of being masculine; it gives a boy the feeling of being powerful, affecting other people's lives.

Drugs
According to the latest research, some 50 per cent of young people will have tried an illegal drug (mostly cannabis) by the time they reach their twenties. Most of

these will either have experimented with such drugs or be using them recreationally. Only a small number (representing about four per cent of young people who have tried drugs) will be considered to have a problem with illegal drugs. In *The Trouble with Boys*, Angela Phillips writes that registered male drug addicts outnumber females by three to one. So although both boys and girls are likely to try drugs, boys are more likely to make drug abuse a 'chosen lifestyle'.

Violence

Physical violence is much more of a vehicle for boys to use to achieve their ends than it is for girls. Angela Phillips writes that boys are four times more likely to be responsible for physical attacks than girls, and they are also far more likely to be victims of attacks than girls. For whatever reason, this suggests that they are much more likely to attack another boy than a girl.

Home Office statistics suggest that 10- to 15-year-old boys are twice as likely to be the victims of violence as girls of the same age and that most attacks on boys happen in a public place, in contrast to incidents of violence against women which occur to a great extent in the home. This suggests that there is a public acceptance of violence by boys against boys and that, in contrast to common belief, girls are actually safer on the streets than boys.

THE NEED FOR SUPPORT

Boys give the impression that they are strong and self-sufficient, and they tend not to say when they are finding things difficult or to ask for help when they need it. However, there is often a contrast between the 'tough' appearance that boys give and what they may be feeling inside. On the one hand, growing numbers of boys may be playing up at school or getting involved in drugs, violence and crime, but on the other hand statistics tell us that:

- 12 per cent of boys are unhappy at secondary school – double the rate of girls;
- the suicide rate among young men between the ages of 15 and 25 rose by over 70 per cent in the 1980s and is five times that of females.

These statistics are offered to suggest how it is particularly important for parents to make clear to their sons that they can turn to their parents – and others – for support whenever they need to, and that they do not have to try to 'tough it out' alone. The earlier parents can start giving these messages to their sons, the more easily their sons will be able to take them in before the 'cool', macho image takes over.

NATURE VERSUS NURTURE

One of the most controversial issues in the discussion about the differences between boys and girls is whether these differences are due to nature – biology – or nurture – the way in which we bring up our children.

Those in favour of the nature point of view argue that girls' advanced verbal skills and boys' advanced spatial skills result from different hormone levels in boys and girls during their mothers' pregnancies and the different ways in which the brain develops and functions in the sexes. Furthermore there is a 'nature' case for why boys do less well than girls at school, and even suggestions that there are biological determinants for why women are better homemakers than men.

The viewpoint at the other end of the spectrum suggests that differences in behaviour between boys and girls can be explained by the way in which they are brought up, and that if boys and girls were treated identically they would turn out the same.

This book recognises that both nature and nurture play their part. It is important to acknowledge biological differences between boys and girls but at the same time, if we are aware of how our society socialises boys and girls, then we can change how we relate to them to enable them each to get the best out of their lives. This book will focus on the way boys are brought up in our society and suggest ways in which parents can respond to their particular needs.

Chapter One

PRESSURES ON BOYS

PARENTAL EXPECTATIONS

OLD HABITS DIE HARD

In the past boys and girls were brought up in accordance with a view of the world that divided life into 'his domain' (the world of work) and 'her domain' (the world of the home). But now we live in a world in which the roles of men and women are up in the air and the old divisions no longer hold true. What does this mean for parents bringing up boys (and girls)?

In the flush of the changes in the 1960s and 1970s newly 'liberated' parents thought they could do it all differently and were shocked when their sons (and daughters) were interested only in the 'old' things they were no longer supposed to like.

Some parents chose egalitarian lifestyles in which they shared earning the money and caring for the children, hoping that their example would encourage their children to be free of the restrictions of gender stereotyping. In other families, fathers may have continued to be the main breadwinner but still consciously chose to be actively involved with their children, unlike the traditional father of the past. However, whatever the family setup, girls continued to play predominantly quiet games with dolls, while boys ran around playing noisily with guns and balls.

The challenge was two-fold: firstly, to understand why the new generation of boys and girls still continued to act in accordance with the old 'rules' that governed the toys they chose, what they played and the activities they enjoyed; and, secondly, to decide what, if anything, to do about it.

CULTURAL IMAGES

Boys and girls receive messages from society with stereotypical images of what it means to be men and women. If the predominant images for boys are men who are always at the centre of the action, then it will be second nature to them to run around wildly making lots of noise (and demanding and expecting all the attention). If the predominant images for girls are women who are nurturing and caring, then it will be second nature to them to play with dolls (and, later on, to want to look after children).

'I always did the ironing at home, never Patricia. I don't think Joanna and John ever saw Patricia ironing. And yet Joanna still came home from playgroup and said: "Mummy does the ironing." That made me realise what a barrier we were up against.' Peter

INTERNALISED IMAGES

Firstly, boys and girls are taught what is expected of them. Next they internalise these gender stereotypes for themselves and come to believe that they are true. They no longer need others to tell them what they are supposed to do. They tell themselves.

'As a teenager I never let anybody know how I was feeling. It never entered my mind that I could have searched out people to talk to about my worries and concerns. I just thought you had to keep them to yourself.

'Now, of course, I realise that was the way boys were taught to be, that it was different for girls.' George

Starting to break out of the gender mould may be difficult for adults, but doing so is even harder for boys and girls. Children mostly want to blend in with the crowd rather than attract attention for being different. There are few rewards outside the home – and probably more forfeits – if they choose to behave outside gender expectations. Boys and girls may feel torn between the messages they get from their parents – that they are free to choose to be the kind of boys and girls they want to be, not limited by their gender – and from pressures from society.

THE MESSAGES SOCIETY SENDS

Before considering how boys can be helped to manage this tension and pressure, it is important to look at the messages they receive from society – and then internalise – about what it means to be male.

'BIG BOYS DON'T CRY'
From a young age boys are discouraged from showing

vulnerable feelings. The reactions from adults towards a girl who falls over and hurts herself are more likely to be supportive and sympathetic than towards a boy, who is more likely to be encouraged to get up again and to carry on without paying attention to either his hurt or his upset. If a boy does cry and is upset, others around him – both young people and adults – may make fun of him and call him derogatory names such as 'sissy'. So he experiences strong pressure not to show any upset feelings.

If a boy is taught that he should not express his sad and vulnerable feelings, it is a short step to no longer being aware of having them. Thus, the boy repeatedly discouraged from showing he is hurt starts to lose awareness that he has even been hurt. He may then act out his own hurt in ways that are destructive to others – with no idea that he is doing it.

'I've noticed that when things don't turn out the way he hoped and he is disappointed, Jordan, ten, is liable to get angry at the first person who crosses his path. It might be me, it might be his brother or sister, or it might even be the cat. He can't seem to see they're his feelings – he has to blame someone else.' Margaret

No longer aware of feeling hurt himself, he loses the ability to notice and empathise when others are feeling hurt. And he loses touch with the effect his actions have on others.

'John doesn't seem to have any idea that his actions affect other people. If I ask him to be quiet or to stop playing a noisy

game he says the words, "Why should I?", but he means, "I'll do what I want." Joanna will listen to my request and take account of my feelings, understanding that they are important.' Patricia

'ACT LIKE A MAN'

From an early age boys are expected to be strong; they are expected to be able to do things on their own and not ask for help. However, it is acceptable for girls to ask for help, and adults are generally more prepared to help them. The expectation that boys are independent is internalised by them from an early age. This results in boys finding difficulty in asking for help and doing their utmost not to admit to, or to deny, any need for help. And this difficulty is carried into adulthood. For example, many men are reluctant to go to see a doctor unless there is absolutely no alternative; rather than seeking help at an early stage, they are more likely to wait until a crisis arises. This covers all areas of a man's life, such as asking a builder-neighbour for help with DIY at home, turning to a colleague at work for help when he doesn't know something, or even admitting to his wife or partner that he doesn't know what to do.

'Real men' – like Batman and Superman – are never afraid, or if they are, they never show their fear. Boys, are not allowed to show their fear, and much of the time adults may forget that they get afraid. Parents may even act in ways that lock boys' fear in tight.

'There are lots of things I like about the way that fathers play physically with their children, but there's one thing I can't stand. You see it in the swimming-pool when they force their

screaming children to go into the water when they're really terrified. The worst example was when I saw a father drop – yes, drop – his young son into the water. The message they are giving their sons is: "It doesn't matter how terrified you are, you're going to have to swallow your terror and do it anyway." I think it's brutal.' Sarah

It's hard when you're a small boy of five years old and you cannot be a child but you have to 'act like a man'.

'YOU HAVE TO DO IT ON YOUR OWN'

Boys have to be 'cool'. As the word suggests, when you are being cool you cannot express warmth and caring for others. This leaves boys with two choices: either to become loners or to seek shelter in the gang, where participants do things together but are not close to each other. In both cases boys stay separate and cut off from others.

'When I was growing up, part of me would really have liked to have had a close friend whom I could talk to, like my sister did. But that wasn't what you did as a boy. You were just supposed to get on with things and not bother about friends and that. But I did miss it at the time and I find it hard to really relax and let myself get close to people now.' George

'THEY'RE ALWAYS LOUD AND ANGRY'

It is generally accepted that boys will be more active and physical than girls, but at the same time boys are often encouraged to show excitement and enthusiasm through physical activity and loud behaviour. How many times have you heard the comment 'He's a real boy' in response to such behaviour? Anger is another feeling that is encouraged in boys, in contrast to girls, who are supposed to be 'nice' and 'kind' – anger is definitely not considered feminine.

Overexcited or angry behaviour in many cases may be punished by adults, who try unsuccessfully to reason with their boys to quieten down. But the punishment can be experienced as a kind of reward (because 'negative' attention is better than no attention). And so the cycle continues.

'WINNER TAKES ALL'

Sports have traditionally been a fundamental area of potential achievement for boys, whether in team games or in solo events. In sports, however, there are always winners and losers; by its very nature, sport encourages competitiveness and exclusion. People might use phrases that say 'Winning isn't everything' or 'It's the playing that counts', but deep down, males in particular (fathers 'teaching' it to their sons) seem to be programmed to be competitive.

There are potential problems with involvement in competitive sports. Firstly, for every winner there is at least one loser and probably more. Also, when picking teams to play football or cricket in the park it is always the same boys who are picked last. This can, of course, be similar for girls, but there is a particular way in which it affects boys. Sport is one of the few areas in which boys are both allowed and encouraged by the peer group to build a positive image of themselves. If a boy is seen as being no good at sport, or if he feels as if he is a sporting failure, the arena in which he can get a good sense of himself is diminished.

'My son loves football and, fortunately for him, he's really good at it. His close friends (all boys) are mostly good at one sport or another, and that seems to be an area where they get lots of recognition – from their friends, from their sports clubs and from the school.

'It's sad that you have to be good at sports to feel good about yourself as a boy. If I hadn't been good at football, I think I would have been really miserable as a child. I feel sorry for the uncoordinated ones.' Henry

Secondly, competitiveness seems to keep boys separated and isolated from one another, rather than connected. This often starts in the sporting arena, despite the cooperation team sports engender, and spreads to other areas of life. You can see this most clearly in men who often seem to be driven by a sense of competitiveness with other men. Men seem to find much more difficulty than women in working cooperatively. Competitiveness seems to be the model that affects male relationships, whether in the boardroom, in the pub or at the park.

'GO FOR IT'

Boys are encouraged to be ambitious in many areas of their lives – because ambition is a quality that is thought to help them get far in life. If boys want to achieve a goal, they are more likely to pursue it single-mindedly than girls, who are likely to be more concerned about the effects of their behaviour on others and not want them to feel excluded.

'If Jordan wants something, nothing will make him change his mind. It doesn't matter what anybody else wants, his needs have to come first. And he's been like that ever since he was tiny. But Geraldine, his older sister, will always defer to other people. When they clash, she's always the one to give in.' Margaret

'BOYS ARE TROUBLE'

When people talk about boys and trouble either they mean that boys are a handful for parents, as opposed to girls, who are 'easy', or they mean that boys 'get into trouble', which means they do things they should not do. And there is a self-fulfilling prophecy about this: if boys hear that they are 'trouble', then they may start to believe it is true and act the part (see Labelling, page 28). As young boys this can mean that they play games that annoy the neighbours, such as ringing their doorbells and running away or swearing at the top of their voices or, when they get older, getting involved in delinquent or criminal acts.

'WOMEN AND CHILDREN FIRST'

When there's a disaster, traditionally the automatic assumption was that women and children should be saved first. They're the ones who went first into the lifeboats of a sinking ship, the ones who were rescued first from a burning house. Men were seen as protectors, and this is men's role – especially in a time of crisis. But somewhere in there another message is received by males: that men's lives are dispensable.

Men train as soldiers and fight in the front line. But when women, in the quest for equal treatment, demand the right to train as fighter pilots, for example, it strikes somewhere at our sensibilities. Killing and being killed are a man's job.

We do not teach boys that they are less important than girls – historically, girls and women have been treated as second class. But if boys are made to feel they are 'dispensable', they will not feel valued as human beings, and this must damage their sense of self-worth. But a boy cannot show such feelings, because he has to be tough – like a soldier.

THE EFFECTS OF THESE MESSAGES

All these messages taken together give a pretty comprehensive picture of what it is like to grow up male. Parents (and, in fact, any adults) may not be aware that this is the way the world appears to boys. If they do not explain to boys that much of how they experience the world and how others react to them is because they are boys, boys will have no idea that they could behave differently or that others could relate to them differently. Thus, they will carry on in the ways they have always learned to behave.

COMBATING THESE EFFECTS

Somewhere, often hidden deep inside most boys, is the potential to be different. When this possibility is revealed to a boy it can make a real difference to the kind of person that he is and could become.

'I was wild as a boy. My parents despaired of me. I bullied children who were younger than me at school, and I didn't do any work in my lessons . . . until we had Mr Jones as our drama teacher. He saw something in me that nobody else had seen. He made English enjoyable and recognised that I could act. And when he saw some good in me, I started to be able to see it too.

'I've never forgotten him. He made a huge difference to my life. I think my life would be a mess if it hadn't been for him. Knowing that I could be good allowed me to calm down inside.' George

It is usually another person who sees something special in a boy – possibly a parent, or another significant adult, or perhaps a friend – and that noticing can be the catalyst for the boy to recognise that he can be different.

The following chapters offer parents ideas for helping boys to see the potential within themselves and learn a wider range of ways of behaving than those permitted by the messages.

Chapter Two

HOW PARENTS CAN HELP SONS OVERCOME THESE PRESSURES

Before we start to consider specific difficulties that parents may have with their sons' behaviour, we need to look at the ways in which parents can most create an environment in the home that will build their sons' self-esteem. This chapter will consider different ways of talking and listening to boys (and girls): ways that can either diminish their self-esteem – and even encourage undesired behaviour – as well as ways that can build self-esteem and encourage the behaviour that parents would like.

THE POWER OF YOUR WORDS AND THOUGHTS

LABELLING
'I was always calling John messy because wherever he went he used to leave a mess behind him. When he took his clothes off, he would leave them lying in a pile wherever he happened to have taken them off. If he had toys or books out in the living-room, he would always leave them wherever they were and would never think about tidying them away. And you should have seen his room . . .

'I then learned about the self-fulfilling nature of labels, and we had a conversation about it. He said that he reckoned he didn't bother about tidying things away because he had learned from me that he was messy. So if I thought he was messy, then he must be messy.

'So we made an agreement. I promised I would stop calling him messy and he promised he would try to take more responsibility for his things. And I'd never have believed it – but the toys, books and clothes never stayed where they had been dropped again. It was like magic.' Patricia

Most parents (and others) use labels as a matter of course. Labels are not used with the intention of creating the very behaviour that parents do not want, but that is often the effect that they have. And then the person being labelled wonders: 'Am I me, or am I my label?'

Labelling can affect a whole group of people as well as individuals. The range of labels that are attached to boys include: noisy, aggressive, demanding, competitive, selfish and naughty. Knowing which comes first, the behaviour or the label, can be difficult, but what is clear is that the labels about boys reinforce their behaviour. New words to describe boys could play a part in helping them to change.

ALTERNATIVES TO LABELS

Parents can avoid the dangers of labelling in a number of ways. Here is a selection of them. (Labelling affects both boys and girls; the alternatives suggested below can be used with both.)

Describing behaviour

Rather than using words to label your children, you can use words to describe their actions and to say how you feel about what they have done.

'Junior was running around and shouting at the top of his voice. Instead of saying, "Stop it. You're so noisy," I remembered to state my feelings and describe his actions: "I get a headache when you run around and shout at the top of your voice." ' Della

This may not lead to an immediate change in Junior's behaviour, but:

• it will avoid the danger of labelling him 'noisy', and labels are dangerous because parents' words are all-powerful: call a child 'noisy' and he may believe he *is* 'noisy'. He will then start to act 'noisy', proving himself to be the very thing that you may want to discourage him from being;
• it is a way of talking to children that helps them develop the understanding that the way they behave affects other people. This is an important understanding because it profoundly affects children's present and future lives, and boys often need help to learn it. Girls may develop empathy in how they interact with others. Boys are more activity-focused and less people-focused and may need help to learn empathy.

So, sharing your feelings and describing children's behaviour can be part of a long-term strategy to help them develop empathy, and not just a short-term strategy to stop unacceptable behaviour.

In the same way, parents can tell their children what they like about them and what they do without using (positive) labels.

'I know it's a funny way of talking, but I've learned to stop saying "good boy" or "helpful boy" when Junior does something that I like, and instead say, "I was pleased that you did your homework rather than just sitting in front of the television," or "I like it when you help clear the table."

'Rather than just fobbing him off with "good boy," I have to really think what I am saying. And as a result he seems to take it in more.

'I've been trying to talk to him like this for a few months, and I think it's making a difference.' Della

Another benefit of descriptions is that when parents describe their children's actions, their children know exactly what they mean, but when parents use labels, such as 'good boy', children may in all honesty not know what their parents are referring to.

Helping children break out of roles
When parents see their children playing roles, such as 'the demanding one' or 'the naughty one' or 'the clever one', it may not be enough just to describe actions instead of using labels. Patterns of behaviour may already be set in place. Parents can do a number of things to help them break out of roles and to learn new ways of behaving:

- Find opportunities to show your child a new picture of himself.

  'Junior, I've noticed how quietly you have been playing since I told you that I've got a terrible headache.' Della

- Put children in situations where they can see themselves differently.

  'Junior was regularly forgetting to feed and walk the dog, so I said to him: "I think you are responsible enough to be in charge of feeding and walking Toffee. If you can't do it, then it's up to you to ensure somebody else does." He's really risen to the occasion and has hardly needed any reminders.' Della

- Let children overhear you speaking positively about them.

  'I was talking on the phone and I made a point of telling my mum that Junior had started to take responsibility for Toffee. He positively beamed when he overheard me – as he was supposed to.' Della

- Model the behaviour you would like to see from your child.

  'When Junior stayed home from school because he wasn't well I said to him: "You know, I had planned to do so many things, and I'm disappointed that I'm not going to be able to. I guess I'll have to make looking after

*you my job for today instead." I really wanted to show
him that I had to make an effort in changing my plans
for him. I hope he'll remember that, when I need a bit of
looking after.'* Della

- Store your child's special moments.

*'Junior came home from school one day and said: "I got
told off for being noisy. The teacher says she'll have to sort
me out if I don't change." Junior had been getting into
trouble at school and I'd prepared myself for such an
occasion. I said to him: "Well, perhaps you were noisy
today, but I remember that time you were quiet all
afternoon when I wasn't well. I know you can keep quiet
if you put your mind to it." '* Della

- State your feelings or expectations, when your
child acts in accordance with an 'old' label.

*'Junior forgot to feed Toffee, so I said to him: "Junior,
you're responsible for Toffee. I expect you to make sure
that he's fed and walked as you agreed." I never thought
it would work, but he replied, "Sorry, Mum," and did
what he had to do.'* Della

As with descriptions, you will need to practise talking
to children in these ways over a period of time. Talking
in these new ways may not come easily. The old words
and phrases will seem to be indelibly printed into your
brain. The new language may feel and sound artificial,
which it will be until you have made it yours. The most
difficult time is when you are just starting out, and that

is the time when you most need encouragement and results.

Some parents find it helps to prepare 'new' phrases in advance so that they will have them ready to use when the situation arises. Other parents say that practising these approaches with a friend, or in a group, really makes a difference.

Just trying to say these phrases once is unlikely to change a child overnight. But offering children new ways of seeing themselves can, over time, help them develop aspects of themselves that were not previously apparent.

HOW PARENTS THINK OF THEIR CHILDREN

'I had learned about the dangers of labelling by the time Karim was born, and I made a point of not labelling him. In my mind I thought about him as "demanding" but never called him "demanding". Similarly, I thought of Jasmine as "independent" but never called her "independent".

'But when it dawned on me that my children responded to the images in my mind rather than the words that came out of my mouth, I realised that I had been screaming my unspoken labels at them.' Aisha

Parents may intend to have equal expectations of their children, but subtle – and not so subtle – differences can creep in. It may help you to stop for a few moments, to close your eyes and get an image of each of your children in turn. What are the words that come into your mind which describe each of them? If you have more than one child, how do the different images compare? What are the aspects of your children that you like and accept, and what are the aspects that you do not like and cannot accept?

The images and expectations of children that parents carry in their minds affect how they relate to and talk to them. It is useful for parents to become aware of what those images and expectations are and to consider if and how they affect their children's behaviour. Then parents can decide whether they really want to try to change what is in their minds so that they can help their children find ways of changing themselves and their behaviour.

FAIR AND REASONABLE EXPECTATIONS

You may feel that your expectations of your children are affected by their gender. Do you have different expectations of your sons and daughters? Girls are often more prepared to help out in the home, whereas boys are often more reluctant, for example. Do you expect your daughters to do more, because it's too much bother to argue with your sons? Do you expect your sons to run around and be noisy and your girls to sit down and get on with things quietly?

Gender is, of course, only one factor that may influence the way you think about your children. Birth order is another area that is important. Often parents are aware of having higher expectations of the eldest child because of that child's greater age and experience. They may also be aware of granting special favours to the youngest child because she or he is the 'baby'.

It is useful to try to become aware of the expectations that you have for your children. It may help to take some time to talk with your partner or a friend about your expectations of your children. What are your expectations? Are your expectations for your children fair and reasonable? How, if at all, would you like to change your expectations for your children?

THE IMPORTANCE OF LISTENING

'Jamie was behaving really badly at school. He was always getting into fights and was a handful for his teachers. I kept getting letters complaining about him and threatening to exclude him if his behaviour did not change. I didn't know what to do: I punished him by grounding him, by stopping his pocket money, and even smacking him. But nothing seemed to work.

'I joined a counselling course as part of my social-work training and through exploring my own childhood and the lack of listening I received, and through learning about listening skills, I thought I might try a new tack with Jamie.

'So one day I asked him how he was feeling and it all tumbled out: he had felt out of control ever since his grandma, who had brought him up for three years, had died. He had never been able to talk about his feelings and deal with his grief. And it came out in impossible, disruptive behaviour. But since I have started listening to him, he has been a changed boy.' William

Listening is an invisible activity, but being listened to well can make a significant difference to how people feel. When boys (and girls) are listened to, their self-esteem goes up. Much of boys' disruptive behaviour is aimed at getting attention. Listening to boys can help them learn to express their difficult feelings – feelings that boys are often discouraged from showing because they are not considered manly – and can play a part in preventing disruptive and antisocial behaviour.

Everybody likes to think of themselves as a good listener, but the reality is that many people do not actually listen that well. Parents have busy lives, and it is all too easy not to give your sons (and daughters) the time they need to talk about whatever is on their minds.

How Boys Talk

When boys talk, they rarely talk about themselves and their feelings. They are much more likely to talk about an area or activity of common interest. Talking about such things is 'safe', whereas talking personally is too threatening for most males. Boys tend to talk 'sideways-on' without looking at one another while focusing on a joint activity, while girls are more able to talk face to face, giving each other their direct attention.

This can pose problems for parents who wish to initiate an important and personal discussion with their sons. Rather than taking the direct approach and saying to your son, 'Let's sit down, we need to talk,' you may be more likely to succeed in striking up a conversation while the two of you are involved in an unrelated activity. This could be when walking somewhere, playing a game together or eating a meal. Your opening words may be, 'By the way, what do you think of . . . ?' If this is met by a blank expression or a refusal to talk, you may follow it up with: 'Well, this is what I think . . .' Various invitations to talk may be required and numerous barriers to responding overcome before a full conversation actually takes place. And remember, too, that a conversation may be initiated on one occasion and may not get a response until later that day or on another day. Relaxed, 'sideways' invitations to talk are more likely to meet with a positive response than the direct approach with all guns blazing. This latter approach may leave you feeling righteously indignant that he has not talked. It is also almost certainly guaranteed to fail to produce the desired conversation.

The following sections introduce ideas to help parents think about listening to their sons (and daughters).

FINDING THE TIME

'Alex, who is 11 years old, hardly talks to me about his day, in contrast to his younger brother and sister, who chatter away constantly. I used to think it was just his temperament.

'However, I went to an evening on "listening to children" at their school and discovered that I might have been the cause of his "temperament"! It wasn't so much that he was quiet, but that I hadn't really been listening to him. I was always busy doing things: looking after the little ones, cooking and cleaning, or telling Alex to be quiet because I was exhausted.

'Of course, I felt dreadful when I realised what I had – or hadn't – been doing, so I resolved to create a time in the day when I could give him proper attention – usually when the others have gone to bed. So now we might sit together

downstairs, or else I spend some time with him when he's in bed. And he's started telling me what he's been doing during his day.

'I've discovered that perhaps he isn't so quiet after all!'
Debbie

Parents' busy lives mean that they often do not have the time or energy to really listen to their children at those moments when their children want to talk about matters of importance to them. Half an ear while you are peeling the carrots may be enough when your son is telling you about his favourite lessons at school, but if he has been bullied he is likely to need your full attention before he will feel able to talk about his worries. Talking 'sideways-on' does not mean giving your son half your attention (while peeling the carrots). It means giving your son your attention in a way that enables him both to feel comfortable and to know that you are listening.

Here are some ideas to help ensure you listen well to your sons (and daughters):

• Make a regular time each day when you can listen to your children, as Debbie did. When brothers and sisters are together, they often compete for your attention. Your sons (and daughters) need to spend time with you alone (as well as being all together), so that they can talk and feel properly listened to. Remember that 'listening time' with your son may be more effective if you appear to be involved in another activity at the same time.
• If your child wants to talk and you do not have the

time or energy to listen at that moment, let him know that you really want to hear what he has to say and arrange a time when you will sit down and listen to him. And, of course, keep to your agreement.

• Interrupt your schedule to listen to your children. Put your children first, and let the tea wait for five or ten minutes, or leave the cooking or cleaning until you have listened to them. Nothing disastrous will happen because of the delay and, as a bonus, your child may feel particularly appreciated because you put him first.

HOW TO LISTEN

'When I used to collect Alex from school, I would ask him what he had done that day. "Nothing, Mum," was his answer and, talking with other parents, I found that they had the same experience with their children.

'At the "listening to children" session, we were introduced to different approaches to talking to children. One idea that really surprised me was that asking children questions could actually make them clam up, that they might experience questions as an interrogation. Instead, we could make a game of what we wanted to know, and then we would be more likely to get the information we wanted.

'So, when I collected Alex from school the next day, I said to him: "Now, let me guess what you did at school today . . ." I made some sensible guesses and some ridiculous ones – which made us both laugh – and within five minutes he had told me all about his day.' Debbie

Some of the following approaches may help you to

encourage your sons (and daughters) to tell you what they are thinking and doing:

• Find a relaxed (and possibly fun) way of asking your children for the information that you want, as Debbie did in the example above. Remember that questions can often be experienced as an interrogation, especially if you are desperate to have the information. It is better to relax and encourage your son just to talk and to forget about getting certain information from him. Paradoxically, the less you feel you must know, the more you are likely to learn!

• When you do ask questions, use open rather than closed questions. Closed questions are questions that lead to the answer 'yes' or 'no': for example, 'Did you hit Andrew at school today?' or 'Did you have a bad day at school?' Such questions invite a one-word answer, leaving the active part of the conversation with you.

Open questions are open-ended and invite the recipient to talk. You might ask, 'What happened at school today?' or 'How was your day at school?' You are less likely to get a one-word answer, which either ends the conversation or requires you to continue talking by asking another question.

• 'What' questions are more productive than 'why' questions. 'Why did you do that?' puts your son on the defensive. 'What' allows for an explanation, as in the question 'What did you do today?'

Reflective Listening
An effective way of encouraging your sons (and

daughters) to talk about what is on their minds, especially when they are feeling upset, is to use a special kind of listening that is often called 'reflective listening'. In the following example of reflective listening, William is using reflective listening to encourage his son, Jamie, to talk:

Jamie comes in from school. William, his father, notices that he looks fed up and says: 'You look as if you've had a bad day.'

'Yeah,' says Jamie.

William: 'Sounds like you don't want to talk about it right now.'

Jamie, testing out his father: 'The teachers shout at me, and I don't want you shouting at me as well.'

William, reflecting back what Jamie has said, in his own words: 'You're not going to tell me because you don't want to be told off again today . . .'

Jamie, opening up a little, says: 'Yes, it's not fair. I always get told off and nobody wants to listen to my side of the story.'

William, reflecting some more: 'Nobody listens to you and you'd like me to.'

'Yes, because I've got so much to tell you,' says Jamie, who is now ready to pour out his story.

'Well, I want to hear it all,' says his father, settling down into his chair, ready to listen.

When parents use words that tell their son that they have heard what he is saying and that they can see how he feels, then he may well feel encouraged to talk. Such listening may not be easy, however, because parents may be encouraging their son to talk about things that are difficult for them to listen to.

Reflective listening does not use questions; it simply uses acknowledging statements that tell the talker in his own words what the listener hears him saying and how he appears to be feeling.

Listening to your son in this way is likely to feel artificial at first, because it is a strange way of talking. However, it can be a particularly useful way of listening to children and young people, because reflective listening requires adults to hold back their comments to what they see and hear, rather than making suggestions because they assume they know what is best for the children. With good listening, your children will not only feel better in themselves but will feel encouraged to find their own solutions to problems.

You may like to practise reflective listening with your partner or a friend, so that you can get the feel of it before you try it with your son. When you first use reflective listening your son may challenge you, and you could respond in the following way, reflecting back his words and explaining the reasons for your new behaviour:

Son: 'You're answering me in a funny way.'

Parent: 'You've noticed that I'm responding differently. I'm actually practising something called "reflective listening," which is supposed to help me learn to listen to you better.'

Son, a little sarcastically: 'So you're going to start listening to me.'

Parent: 'So you've noticed I could listen to you better.'
And so on.

Reflective listening allows talkers to get to the bottom of their feelings. When they have reached the end of what they want to say, they may need to be moved on, perhaps with a question or the chance to think with you as to what action they might want to take. They may, of course, just feel better for having talked and been listened to and may not want to take any further action.

Beware of offering suggestions and solutions to your sons (and daughters), especially if they have not asked for them. It is probably better not to give them, or to ask if they would like to hear your thoughts.

Chapter Three

BOYS' BEHAVIOUR: PROBLEMS AND SOLUTIONS

EMOTIONS AND AFFECTION

As Chapter One showed, boys face many messages and expectations which determine much of their behaviour. Many of the pressures cause boys to become isolated – unable to show their vulnerability or to turn to others for support. In the process of playing the part of 'the man', boys can get cut off from other people.

Because these messages are not generally recognised and understood, the way in which boys behave is assumed to be 'normal'. So 'real boys' are assumed to behave in stereotypically macho ways, and the distance that keeps boys and men apart (from each other, and also from girls and women, other than in intimate and sexual relationships) is assumed to be natural. It is also easy to assume that, in later life, men are unable to manage their own and others' feelings because that is the way they are. However, boys (and men) are capable of showing a full range of emotions and behaving in a wide variety of ways.

Here are some ideas on how parents can create an environment that will encourage boys both to feel and express all their emotions – rather than repressing the vulnerable parts of themselves – and be physically and emotionally close to others.

CREATING A SAFE SPACE AT HOME

You may find it helpful to think of two worlds for boys, the outside world and the world of the home. The outside world will demand conformity from boys to follow the rules laid down by the messages. If a boy goes against them, he is likely to suffer ridicule and humiliation. Parents can recognise this, while at the same time creating a safe space for their sons at home in which they can explore and share their softer, more vulnerable and affectionate sides.

How can parents do this?

- *through their own example*: sharing their feelings with their sons. A father can particularly influence his son in this area. How a father deals with his feelings will guide his son in how he deals with *his* feelings. Mothers, of course, also influence their sons and, if their sons do not live with or have little contact with their father, they can help their sons by involving them with male friends and members of the family who are open about their feelings.
- *by acknowledging boys' feelings*: when a boy comes home upset about his day – perhaps at school – then an acknowledging response – 'I can see that was upsetting' or 'I wouldn't have liked that either' – is generally more helpful than saying something like 'Don't make such a fuss' or 'I haven't got time for such stories'.
- *by recognising that home is a place to let your hair*

down: a boy needs to be able to let his hair down at home, to be himself and not have to live up to some image of what it means to be male. A boy is more likely to become a strong man, with a solid sense of who he is, if he is allowed to explore and share this inner part of himself. Men with a tough exterior may not be as strong as they appear and may find it particularly hard to deal with uncomfortable feelings when they surface.

PHYSICAL CLOSENESS WITH BOYS

Boys learn from an early age that hugging and physical closeness is not OK. Parents tend to stop hugging and having physical contact with their sons at a younger age than with their daughters – perhaps partly because they sense their sons' (and their own) discomfort with physical contact, and partly because they feel they need to prepare their sons for the world they are going to grow in to.

But boys need hugs as much as, if not more than, girls as society starves them of physical contact. All humans (male and female) thrive on physical closeness, and hugs are one way of giving and receiving love. If hugging has stopped being a part of the physical contact between parents and their sons, what can parents do to try to reintroduce such closeness?

• Do not force hugs on your sons as that will put them off physical closeness even more.
• Make a game of it. Pretend to kiss them lightly or to touch them or hug them just a little more than they

feel is acceptable, with a view to getting them to laugh off some of their embarrassment. As they (and you) laugh off the embarrassment, they (and you) may get more relaxed about touch.

• Remember that boys get closeness in other ways than hugs and kisses. Physical closeness is a key part of wrestling and play fighting. So you could take your shoes off and join in the action (see pages 56–9). At the end of a good 'fight' you may sit and cuddle closely with 'the enemy' as you wind down from the exertion.

Boys need help to reconnect with physical closeness. The dominant culture discourages physical closeness for boys. Your role as a parent is to try to open a window (and keep it open) for your son to be able to be close to you. You may succeed in reintroducing physical closeness at home, but remember the harshness of the outside world on boys and do not expect them to go hugging down the street!

PHYSICAL ENERGY

Boys, in particular, seem to have so much physical energy that they can hardly sit still.

'When Jordan watches the television, he may be sitting quietly for a few minutes, but then he will be up on his feet, moving round the room wanting to kick a ball, or lying down and fiddling with a cupboard handle with his feet or playing around with something in his hands. It's as if his body needs to be doing something while his mind focuses. And I've

tested him to see if he is taking in what he is watching – and I'm surprised that on the whole he is able to answer my questions correctly!

'Geraldine will just sit down and watch a programme like a "normal" human being.' Margaret

Nowadays, parents are concerned for their children's safety outside the home. They are fearful of the dangers posed by the number and speed of cars and of strangers whom they fear may abuse their children – though in fact statistics show that the number of children hurt by strangers has not increased over the last 20 years; it is just that media coverage is more immediate and widespread. As a result, children are given less freedom to play outside on their own.

In the past, a boy could go to a park or play in fields on his own and run off some of his excess energy. But now parents may keep boys (and girls) indoors if they are not able to go out with them; they can only take them out to play when their other tasks are completed or can be left. The result is that boys spend more time cooped up inside their homes becoming couch potatoes as they watch television and play computer games. More and more of them do not get the exercise they need to keep healthy, and frustration builds up between parents and their children as they have less space and time apart from each other.

'When I was young I spent all my free time out in the open. Even if it was raining my mother would let me muck around with my friends outdoors. We didn't do anything particularly constructive; it's just that we were away from

the adults and could do exactly what we wanted.

'But now our children are allowed outside only with supervision; they have no freedom and they do not experience independence the way we did.' George

HOW TO COPE WITH EXCESS ENERGY

There are no easy answers to this. This is one of the stresses of living in our modern society, which undervalues the importance of creating safe play spaces close to the home and instead allows cars to dominate our streets. Sadly, many parents find that the role of chauffeur takes up more of their time than they would wish (ironically adding to the problem of traffic on the roads). You may like to bear the following points in mind.

• Children need the opportunity to exercise regularly and let off steam. If they are too young to go to a playground or park on their own, then you could regularly schedule a time to take them – after school, for example – and you may like to take them with a few friends so that they can all play together. If they are old enough to be allowed out on their own, you may be comfortable with them playing outside so long as you know when they will come home.
• Encourage your children – if they need any encouragement – to participate in physical or sporting activities. Clubs and leisure centres offer many such activities for young people. Remember that participation in the activity is most important, not being successful or being 'the best'. If your son is not particularly successful at an activity, he may need

greater encouragement to continue participating if he enjoys it, or you may wish to help him to find something else that he might get satisfaction from. Cubs and Scouts (and Brownies and Guides for girls) and Woodcraft Folk all provide a range of activities that your sons might enjoy.

• Finding an activity for children will be good for you, too. You need a break from them as much as they need a break from you. An outside activity will get them out from under your feet, and they will enjoy doing things away from you when they have overcome any initial fears of separation. You are likely to value the peace, even if it is only to sit on a bench keeping an eye out on the children, talking to other parents or reading the paper.

AGGRESSION AND FIGHTING

FIGHTING GAMES

'My mother didn't allow us to have guns in the house. And she stopped us playing Cowboys and Indians and other fighting games as well. Now that seems to form a major part of what Peter wants to do with his friends. The technology may be more sophisticated in that they shoot at each other with laser guns rather than bows and arrows, but the game is the same. I don't approve, but I couldn't stop them the way my mother seemed able to stop us.' George

Many schools have a policy that their pupils are not allowed to bring toy weapons on to the premises. However, this doesn't prevent the pupils, mostly boys, from making them in the classroom (out of Lego or wood), using pencils or sticks as amunition or, failing that, just pointing their fingers at each other and saying: 'Bang, bang. You're dead.' And it's often the same at home. Boys seem to be drawn to playing such games and, whether you like it or not, they will find a way to play these games even if means just pointing their fingers in imitation of a gun.

In the past, parental injunction may have stopped children from playing these games and doing the things that parents did not like. Nowadays it is much harder for parents to influence their children's games. With a staple diet of male fighting images on television, it is perhaps no wonder that boys want to play so many fighting games (see Supporting Boys in Their Friendships on page 95 for a brief discussion on the meaning of playing with guns). Girls, however, who have a completely different set of images held up to them, have hardly any interest in these games.

ROUGH-AND-TUMBLE

Boys are much more likely than girls to resort to rough-and-tumble play. To adults this may appear to be a game that could end in tears, but boys are unlikely to be stopped from playing in this way. It's as if it's in their blood.

'Graham and Brian constantly fight each other but not in any vicious kind of way. Sometimes one or other of them will come running to me in tears, telling a story of what the other one did to him, but most of the time they laugh their way through their fights and come out the other end – either

having sorted out the disagreement that started them fighting or having forgotten about it.

'I used to try to stop them from playing in this way, but I've learned that I can't – they'll do it anyway – and that it seems to be part of their way of being brothers together. I don't think I'll ever get to like it though.' Julia

FIGHTING

Many parents feel uncomfortable with their sons fighting and find difficulty in distinguishing between 'play' fights and 'real' fights. When they reflect on this, however, parents often say that the quality of children's fighting is different when no adults are present from when they are. Somehow children seem to resolve their fights more successfully when they are alone but put on a performance, with increased volume and harder hitting, when their parents are in the room. And parents usually respond by getting drawn into trying to sort out children's fights, rather than leaving the room to let them get on with things (see below for thoughts on how you can respond).

It is helpful to make the distinction between 'play' fighting and 'real' fighting. Although play fighting may arise out of a conflict between two children, it's as if a part of them recognises that this is a game and that they do not want to hurt the other. Unwritten rules of play fighting govern the way children fight, and they know not to overstep the bounds and really hurt the other participant. Laughter often characterises play fighting.

Real fighting may result when somebody or something triggers such strong feelings in a boy (or girl) that he cannot control himself and just hits out, as if a monster is raging unchecked within him. Although both girls and boys 'lose it' at times, boys are more regularly involved in fights than are girls. A number of reasons could be behind this, for example:

- girls have a higher threshold of self-control and so 'lose it' less often;
- girls have different ways of hitting out: by using words, for example.

But, as with play fighting, parents seem to see red when their children fight, and their strongest impulse is to jump in and stop the fight. Parents may have a fantasy image of how they want their children to be the best of friends with their brothers and sisters and, when their children fight, this image is destroyed. Whatever the reason, this is often an area of great difficulty for parents.

A fear mothers may carry is that if their sons fight as children, they may become violent (and abusive) men. However, fighting is part of the repertoire of many boys (and some girls), and because they fight when young does not mean that they will grow into violent adults. Repressed anger is, in fact, more likely to lead to men becoming violent because they cannot control the force of their anger, rather than fighting in childhood. Boys (and girls) who fight need parents who can help them draw the line when the fighting gets out of control and others may get hurt. Parents should help them learn to control their aggressive feelings rather than being controlled by them.

SOLUTIONS TO THE PROBLEMS OF FIGHTING

You can approach your boys' needs to play physically and to fight with ideas based on the following principles: it is helpful to understand the frustrations that boys (and girls) may feel which may lead them to fight and be aggressive if they are not acknowledged and dealt with; and it is generally better for boys (and girls) to get their feelings of anger and aggression out of their systems rather than to suppress them. These ideas are broken down into three sections:

- *play fighting*, in which parents specifically help their sons (and daughters) to express their anger and frustration in play;
- *real fighting*, which includes tips on when (and when not) and how (and how not) to intervene when children are fighting 'for real';
- *winding down*: helping boys (and girls) to calm down after they have got worked up and excited after being involved in play, or real, fighting.

Play fighting

Living in society is a frustrating business for boys (and girls). They have to spend so much time fitting in with other (mostly larger) people's schedules that they often feel a sense of frustration and irritation that they cannot have things their own way. Parents may feel that if they spend regular time with their children doing the things their children want, then their children will be satisfied with this and not demand any more. The irony is, however, that the more time parents give their children, the more time their children want and expect.

It is as if parents can never give them enough!

Play fighting is a way of playing with your children and helping them to let out any feelings of anger and frustration. You can set up a play fight, for example, when children come home from school, or you can schedule an impromptu play fight when tensions seem to be rising and your child seems to need a release.

'Billy used to love play fighting. We had a kind of ritual. We'd get out the cushions, take off our shoes and then get down on the floor. And then he'd start hitting me with a cushion. I would fall around in mock agony, oohing and aahing as if he'd caused me lots of damage. He would laugh and laugh, and keep on hitting me. I used to try to hit him back, in among the blows as they were raining down on me. That was important because otherwise he'd get annoyed and say: "You're not trying." He didn't like that. I got quite good at falling about and getting him to laugh and also learned to put up enough resistance to make it real enough for him.

'When he has friends round they like to have pillow fights. I've seen Billy use what he has learned from our play fights. And sometimes I join in and allow myself to be the target. It lets them laugh and laugh, which helps to drain away any tension they may be carrying. I think they then get on better and fight less.' Jessica

Play fighting aims to help children release the tensions that are stored within them, and gales of laughter are often a sign that a play fight is going well. It is helpful for adults to be the targets and to play act as if the blows are seriously damaging, as Jessica does in the example above. At the same time it is useful to set up rules to ensure that nobody gets hurt, because play fighting is not about damaging one another – it is about releasing tension. Rules can include:

- take off shoes before the play fight begins;
- no hair-pulling or scratching;
- hit only with cushion or balloon (or whatever soft implement is being used).

Real fighting

There will always be occasions when children will fight and tensions between siblings are often the flashpoint. Boys in particular seem to need the physicality of fighting, perhaps in part because they are so often starved of hugs and physical closeness. (You can help balance this by encouraging your sons to feel comfortable with hugs, although this may not be easy because boys may be reluctant to be hugged from quite an early age – see page 47). When fights break out, here are some thoughts that can guide you in your response.

- Avoid taking the role of referee or policeman when children fight: 'once a policeman, always a policeman.' Children will continually come to you to sort out their disagreements, and at least one of them will always be unhappy with your response. Rather than intervening in the detail of the conflict, acknowledge their feelings – 'You both look really angry' or 'You both want that toy on your own' – and, when the tension has decreased, encourage them to find their own resolution to the conflict – 'You've got a difficult problem there, *and* I bet the two of you can sort it out.'

• Similarly, actively encourage your children to sort out their own fights rather than thinking that you always have to intervene. The quality of children's fights is often different in front of adults, when they expect an intervention. If the children are not doing any serious damage to each other, you may wish to leave the room or, if you are able to, sit quietly in the corner and let them sort out their differences by themselves. If the fight seems to be getting out of hand, then you might intervene, but to stop the fight rather than to get involved in the issues. So, for example, you might say, 'Stop. This looks nasty. Go to your rooms until you've both calmed down. Then we'll talk.'

• You may need rules to guide the children in their disputes. You can ensure that a younger child knows that he or she is not allowed to interfere with an older child's things. A bigger and older son needs to know that he is not allowed to pick fights with a younger child (particularly a girl) which he will always win. In this case you are not taking the referee or policeman role, but you are giving your children tools to help them deal with inequality between them, very useful tools for use in wider society.

Winding down
After expending lots of energy, whether in play fights or real fights, boys (and girls) need time to wind down. Otherwise they are likely to continue to be hyperactive and not be able to calm down. Parents can help their

sons to wind down by sitting with them, possibly stroking them and talking with them quietly until they are calmer and more relaxed. Fathers are often responsible for 'winding children up' because of the extra energy they put into their play, but they are often unaware that winding down needs to be an integral part of these games.

DISCIPLINE AND BOUNDARIES

One of the biggest problems that parents have with their sons (and daughters) is setting limits or boundaries and saying no and sticking to it. Many reasons can be put forward for this. Here are two of them:

• In the past there was more respect for authority, not just the authority of parents but for authority in general – the teacher, the policeman, the social worker and the judge, for example. Now, many of the figures of authority have been challenged and found wanting. So when parents act with authority, their sons (and daughters) are much more likely to challenge them than they would have challenged their own parents.

'When I was a child I did what my parents said. I hardly ever questioned their word. But when I tell my children what needs to be done, they hardly ever do it without challenging me. And I hear other parents saying: "My children say things that I would never have dared say to my parents." It's not that any of us are doing anything wrong; it's more that the climate of the times has changed.' Stephen

- So many conflicting views about how to bring up children and so many different styles of parenting are on offer that many parents have lost confidence in themselves as parents. At least in the era of the authoritarian style of parenting, when children were supposed to be seen and not heard, parents received a unified message that they could follow or not, as the case may be. Today, a range of different approaches to parenting are offered, from permissive to authoritarian, and parents are often fearful of drawing, or uncertain where to draw, the line on their children's behaviour.

Many parents find that their sons push the limits harder than their daughters, so parental struggles with enforcing discipline and boundaries are often more acute with boys.

DISCIPLINE AND PUNISHMENT

Discipline is a difficult subject to discuss because people understand so many different things by the word. The biggest problem with the term 'discipline' is that it is often used interchangeably with 'punishment'. When people say 'He needs disciplining' what they usually mean is 'He needs to be punished'.

Children learn discipline from others. And as they experience discipline from the outside, they are then able to internalise it and learn self-discipline 'on the inside'.

'I came to collect John from his friend's the other day and was surprised by his response. I said: "John, I need to take you straight home, as I'm going out tonight and haven't

much time – you may remember, we talked about it this morning."

'John really wanted to stay and play with his friend some more, but he knew that he had to come straight away as I was going out in the evening – and he did. Normally he tries every trick in the book to stay and play a bit longer. I was surprised – and impressed – by his response.'
Geraldine

In this example John shows self-discipline. A part of him wants to stay and play with his friend, but he has learned that his mother has her own needs that he is able, in this case, to allow to take precedence over his. If John had not come quietly with his mother what might she have done?

'Well, I would have done one of two things. If I could have stayed calm enough inside I would have repeated my request and maybe acknowledged his feelings. But knowing me, I wouldn't have been able to repeat it a third time without raising my voice and telling him to come now. *And, if I'm honest, I might have threatened or bribed him to make him come.'* Geraldine

And that's probably what many parents would do! When children do not obey, they respond by punishing.

The questions for parents are:

• how do you teach your children self-discipline – an important skill that will serve them well throughout their lives – and
• how do you enforce boundaries when you set

them – in a way that both teaches discipline and gets the limit met?

TEACHING CHILDREN SELF-DISCIPLINE

Perhaps surprisingly, children learn their most effective lessons about self-discipline at times of peace and harmony. It is generally recognised that we all learn new things best when we are feeling relaxed and good about ourselves, just how parents (and their children) are *not* feeling at times of crisis and conflict.

Children want to please their parents. This is worth repeating because it's something that parents easily forget in the stresses and strains and ups and downs of daily parenting. *Children really do want to please their parents.* And if parents give their children positive 'strokes' for the things that they approve of, their children are likely to repeat those pieces of behaviour.

'Ben would always come home a little later than agreed, maybe ten or fifteen minutes. For some reason he seemed to need to go against what we had agreed, but it wasn't worth making a big fuss out of it.

'One day he came home from the park on time, and fortunately I noticed. I told him how much it meant to me because I didn't have that little flutter of anxiety about whether something might have happened to him. He seemed surprised by my response and spent some time thinking about it.

'A few days later he said to me: "You know I was home on time that day and you told me how pleased you were. Well, I always thought you were trying to boss me around by telling

me when to come home – and I suppose that's why I was always late. But if you're not trying to boss me around, then I can come home on time if I want to." ' Rachael

Rachael's appreciation of Ben allowed him to work out in his mind why he had a problem with being on time. If his mother had just focused on his lateness, her critical comments would probably just have confirmed him in his behaviour. But because she appreciated him (for what she liked), he was able to think things through afresh.

If parents can tell their children what they like about them and what they do, then they have gone half-way towards having their children do it, without fights and battles. Other ways of talking to children were described in the previous chapter – such as describing behaviour rather than labelling the person, and acknowledging children's feelings. Talking to children in these ways will help them learn self-discipline and is likely to boost a spirit of cooperation between you.

BOUNDARIES

All children need boundaries. Boundaries give a child a sense of security. Some parents may feel reluctant to impose boundaries, not wanting to be mean. But children actually need what is called 'authoritative parenting' in which firm rules are set within a climate of warmth and affection.

There will always be times when it is appropriate for parents to negotiate with their sons (and daughters). Knowing when to negotiate and when to set limits and say 'no' is the second part of teaching children about discipline. And the way you set limits will affect the way your children respond. Your goal could be to set limits without needing to resort to punishment, for two reasons: firstly, children and young people deserve to be treated with respect, and punishment (as opposed to setting limits and teaching discipline) tells children that you will make them do what you want them to do because of your greater size and power; and secondly, because if you punish (or bribe) children to do something that they don't want to do, then they are likely to expect a bigger punishment (or bribe) the next time. Thus, your smacks may have to get harder or more frequent and your bribes may need to get bigger and better as your children grow older. Far better to avoid carrots and sticks and practise setting limits and negotiating from the start (see also page 68, When There is No Alternative to Punishment).

Here are some ideas to help you with setting boundaries:

• It is the task of parents to set boundaries and the task of children to push against them. Some children, often boys, push the boundaries harder than others and, if anything, they need boundaries more than those who do not push so hard.
• How often should parents say 'no'? Many parents say 'no' instinctively and when they think about it afterwards, realise that on some occasions they did not mean 'no'. They then change their 'no' to a 'yes'. This is confusing for children, for they may learn that when, for example, Mum says 'no', with a little bit of

pushing they can get her to change her mind to 'yes'. In this way parents actually encourage their children to challenge their 'no'. Far better to think about the matter first and say 'no' only when you really mean it. Children will then know better where they stand, although they are unlikely to say, 'Thank you for saying "no" to me. I'm so pleased!' Rather, disappointment and upset are the more likely responses, and parents can acknowledge their disappointment *and* repeat the 'no': 'I know you really want to stay and play with your friends *and* I said you have to come home now!'

• When you say 'no' it is important that you mean it. If part of your tone or your body communicates 'maybe', children will hear that and will push for clarity – either to get you to change your mind or to hear you reinforce your 'no'. Say 'no' with your whole body.

• When you are setting a boundary that involves protecting children from danger, then you may wish to set the boundary a little way off the final point, so that if they stretch the boundary further than agreed they will still be within safe margins.

'I want Robin to be home from the park before it's dark. So rather than saying he has to be home at dusk, I set a time when I know it will still be light, so if he is late – and he usually is – he'll still be home before it's dark.' Maureen

• When should parents say 'no'? Parents need to say 'no' in situations of danger when there is no time to negotiate, such as when a child is about to run out into a busy road. Parents also need to recognise their own needs.

'It took me a long time to learn the lesson that I needed to take my own needs into account. When the children asked me for something, I always tried to avoid saying "no" unless I really had to. But what that meant was that I often did things unwillingly with and for them. And I realised that usually my unwillingness – which turned into resentment – often leaked out and spoiled the very thing that I had done for them.

'One example was taking them for a trip when I really didn't want to. We all had a nice time, but I spoiled it by shouting at them non-stop on the way home. They hadn't done anything wrong; it was all because I hadn't wanted to go in the first place. Another example was cooking them something special when I didn't have the energy to do more than mix a packet of soup.

'But since I've learned to trust my own intuition and say "no" when I need to, my "yes" is more generous and I think I am a happier person for it – and so, of course, are the children.' Maureen

• Children need to learn both to accept the authority of their parents and to learn the skills of negotiation, to help them in all their relationships, current and future. Parents need to search their minds to see if they mean 'no' and then say it. Otherwise they can negotiate with their children over whatever it is they want.

'The boys wanted to stay up late in the holidays and watch a film on the television. I said that was fine with me so long

as the living-room was cleared up by nine o'clock the next morning when friends were coming round. They decided that they would watch the film in sleeping-bags, and then go to bed to sleep through the night and have a lie-in in the morning. They were pleased with the solution, particularly because it was their own, and I was pleased that the room would be clear for me.' Maureen

In a negotiation it is useful to remember that the solutions that children come up with may not be the ones that you would have chosen, but the fact that they found them means that they are all the likelier to want them to work.

• Keep the 'no's' to a minimum. For young children a question such as 'What do you want for breakfast?' may lead to an answer to which you feel you have to say 'no', such as 'Some sweets' or 'A bar of chocolate'. A question offering a limited choice, such as 'Do you want cornflakes or crispies for breakfast?' will avoid such a response and offers a helpful framework for young children. As children grow older they are able to handle larger and larger choices.

Negotiation will be much more the order of the day with teenagers. Whatever the age of your children, however, say 'no' only when there are no alternatives.

• If you have been using rewards and punishments and would like to change your approach to a firm limits and negotiation one, then you will need to explain to your children how you plan to do things differently in future. Explaining the change will give your child the chance to understand why you are behaving differently and not confuse him by your behaviour. He may well resist your new approach – because he, quite sensibly, wants his rewards – but you can gently, and firmly, insist that when you say 'no' you mean 'no'.

WHEN THERE IS NO ALTERNATIVE TO PUNISHMENT

However good you get at setting limits and sticking to them firmly, there will always be times when your children will not accept your limits, and when you feel you have no alternative but to punish them. Here are some more thoughts to help avoid deadlock and to use punishment when necessary:

• Rather than saying 'You can't watch television until you've done your homework' – that is, threatening a sanction if a certain action is not undertaken – it is more useful to turn the threat round into a positive statement: 'You can watch television when you've done your homework.' Such a phrase is experienced as less confrontational than the equivalent threat, and almost as an invitation to do the necessary activity to get the reward. Sentences starting with 'Unless you . . .' or 'If you don't . . .' can always be turned into positive statements.
• If you say you will do something as a punishment, then it is important to carry it out. If you say to a child that he can have pudding only if he eats his main course, then you only give him desert if he actually eats his main course. A child on the receiving end of empty threats is unlikely to take future threats seriously. Consistency in saying only what you

mean – and then doing it – is important.

• Make a punishment fit the crime. Thus, if your child breaks a valuable item in the house, there is a logic to making him pay for it by stopping his pocket money for a certain number of weeks. A similar logic prevails in grounding a child who continually arrives home later than the agreed time. If there is little relationship between the punishment and the crime (both in kind and in severity), then your child is likely to feel particularly resentful towards you. Often he will know he has done wrong and expect punishment, even though he does not admit it and protests vehemently.

• If you feel you are going to overreact and may do something you might later regret, you can always leave the room for a few minutes – what you might call 'time out for parents'. If you tell your child that you feel so angry that you need to take a few minutes to calm down, this may help him calm down as well and be more understanding of your upset, because you have chosen not to take it out on him.

LACKING SELF-RELIANCE, AVOIDING RESPONSIBILITY

LACKING SELF-RELIANCE

Something that makes parenting girls easier than parenting boys is that girls seem to understand and learn the concepts of independence and self-sufficiency more easily. Girls are more likely to curl up with a book or amuse themselves with a game – whether on their own or with friends – than boys, who are more likely to seek out their parents – or any other adult – to ask for their attention, saying, 'I don't know what to do' or 'I'm bored'. Such phrases are guaranteed to get parents either to make lots of 'helpful' suggestions as to what their sons could do – most of which are met by cries of, 'No, that's no good' – or to shout at them. Both responses perpetuate the complaints rather than changing them.

At this point it may be helpful to clarify the difference between this 'demanding' behaviour and what was said in Chapter One about boys needing to be independent and hiding any signs of vulnerability. In this situation boys are demanding attention, not showing their vulnerability. Boys (and girls) who demand attention in this way are not being 'open' and 'vulnerable'; rather, they may seem 'irritating' and 'annoying'.

If children are able to get on with things on their own, not only does this ease parents' lives but it also gives children the beginnings of an important skill: being able to apply themselves to the task at hand without needing to call for help when things get difficult. This is a key skill in developing maturity and greater independence: being able to fend for yourself and take on greater responsibility.

Here are some ideas that may help you think about responding in new ways to sons who seem to need your help constantly.

• For a boy who is bored and doesn't know what to do, you can acknowledge his feelings by saying, for example, 'I can see how fed up you are. None of your friends are free. You think the programmes on the TV are rubbish and your toys are boring.' Acknowledging his feelings may enable him to feel that you care about him and how he feels. This will help him, even though it is unlikely to be the magic solution to solve his boredom.

• You may feel frustrated and irritated by his behaviour, but you can say to yourself: 'The boredom is *his* problem to solve, not mine, so I'll put my feelings of frustration and irritation aside and leave *him* to work out what *he* is going to do, possibly offering *him* the option of coming to talk to me if *he* wants to, and get on with what *I* want to do.' In other words, you allow him to take responsibility for himself rather than feeling that it's always your – the parent's – responsibility to ensure that your sons are occupied and contented.

AVOIDING RESPONSIBILITY

'If John breaks something, his immediate response is: "It wasn't my fault." I used to think this was an indication that he was scared of being told off by me, but now I think it's more a sign that he doesn't think he has to take responsibility for his actions when things don't turn out well.

'If he loses something at home, it's always "somebody else's" fault and "somebody else" ought to find it. If he wants something, his automatic reaction is to ask "somebody else" to get it for him, even if it would be easier for him to get it. In his mind "somebody else" seems to be there to serve him and take the rap for anything that goes wrong.' Patricia

And that 'somebody else' is invariably his mum, the main carer. Not only is it infuriating to be ordered around as if you were your son's slave, but it is all the more so in these times when women are trying to get men (and boys) to be more sensitive to and respectful of their needs.

Girls seem to find it easier to learn to take responsibility for their things. Perhaps this comes in part from the games they play with their peers, which include more 'give and take', perhaps in part from the greater expectations that parents have of their daughters to help out at home, and perhaps in part from following the example of their mothers (and the images of women around them) taking responsibility for the home. Whatever the cause, many parents see a gap between boys' and girls' sense of responsibility.

Boys similarly seem to have less awareness of and empathy with other people's feelings and needs. This probably results from similar causes: activity-focused games rather than games that involve give and take with others, lower parental expectations of them and the example set by both the men and the images of men that surround them. Parents can easily feel angry and frustrated towards their sons because of their relative lack of empathy compared with their daughters.

How can parents encourage their sons to take more responsibility for themselves?

Parents need to give their sons (and daughters) increasing responsibility as they grow older. If you decide to take responsibility only for what is yours and allow your sons to take responsibility for what is theirs, then they have the opportunity to learn to be responsible for themselves. To help you decide who should be taking responsibility in a given situation, ask yourself whose problem it is, as Maureen does in the following example. The answer here is Luke's, so she gives him the responsibility to solve the problem.

'Luke could never find his school things in the morning. I used to rush around looking for him and then decided it was ridiculous. I told him I wasn't going to do it any more. I don't think he believed me because the next few days he couldn't find his things, as usual, but I sat at the breakfast table and didn't move. And since then he's always found his things in the morning.' Maureen

Of course, life isn't made up of situations that are always clear cut. Other questions that you may need to ask yourself after 'Whose problem is it?' may be:

- *Whose needs need meeting first?* – if two or more people have a problem in a particular situation – or
- *Can I live with the consequences?* – of allowing my son to learn from the consequences of his actions: for example, few parents will allow their young children to cross a busy road as a way of learning road safety, whereas many will allow their children to learn that if they spend all their pocket money when they are given it, they will have nothing left for the rest of the week.

Rather than having arguments and labelling your son irresponsible (and confirming him in his behaviour), you can ask him questions that will help him think about what he needs to do:

- What do you need to take with you?
- Where else could you look for it?
- How will you do that?

Your son is unlikely to change overnight, but over time, as he practises acting responsibly, he will learn to take more responsibility. The younger you start with giving children responsibility for aspects of their own lives, the more easily they will learn it for future years, although this is often a difficult lesson for many children and causes much grief for many parents.

COMPETITIVENESS

'I remember as a child competing desperately with my father in everything that we did. I didn't have a chance against him, of course, because he was so much bigger and stronger. I also competed against all my peers – I wanted to be the best. It wasn't enough to do my best, I had to be the best. I never made it, of course, and I still feel as if I'm struggling to be the best.

'When I look at Jason, I see him comparing himself with and competing against the other children of his age. I've tried to bring him up not to do that – as a reaction against my own experience – but I don't seem to have had much influence. However, I feel I have been much more successful with Joanna, who certainly measures herself against her friends but doesn't seem to be all-consumed by the sense of competition.' Henry

All children want to win; some want to win more than others. If you compare your sons with your daughters, you may have a sense that boys are that bit more determined to win than girls. Not necessarily because they are any better, but because the competition – or the fear of failure or losing face – is that much more important to them. Girls may get upset about not succeeding but are less likely to show or act out their disappointment in the way that boys do. And they will often play a game for companionship and not be particularly concerned about winning or losing.

Boys' extra competitiveness poses problems for parents. In playing games within the family, boys may get more upset when they do not win, act out their disappointment and thus spoil the game by leaving a sour taste in their parents' mouths. A game of football between father and son may finish smoothly when the son wins, but if the father wins there may be a period (of extra time!) during which the son is driven – by the raging monster of unfairness and disappointment inside him – to kick, scream, shout and complain at his father. The son feels a desperate need either to extend the game so that he can win in the end or to try to exorcise that feeling of having been destroyed through losing by throwing the full force of the feeling at his father.

In the safety of the home, boys may feel able to show the depths of their upset and disappointment. This is less likely outside the home – as such behaviour does not fit the image of what boys are supposed to do – when their sense of competitiveness may result in them acting 'cool' when they don't win, as if they didn't really lose or don't care. In the case of sports, for example, there may be some way of explaining away the reason why they lost: 'the referee was biased', 'the other team played dirty' or just 'we deserved to win'. When it comes to underachievement at school, compared with girls, they claim that 'we weren't really competing anyway', which enables them to hang on to their picture of being cleverer than girls despite their results.

How can parents help the competitive ones among their children come to terms with losing?

• Children cannot win too much, especially boys with their competitive spirit. Rather than trying to squash their desire to win out of them, you can let them get winning out of their systems.

When playing games, a parent's role is to test the child and mostly to let him (or her) win whatever game they are playing. Boys (and girls) need to win because it helps them to feel on top of the world. So much of their lives is spent fitting into the adult world that winning in a game against an adult gives them an opportunity to triumph for a change. As with play fighting, if you can lose with good humour and make a show of massive disappointment, a son will find his victory all the more enjoyable, and it will bring forth much laughter.

• Parents need to challenge their children so that they are pushed to their limit, but one object of a game for parents is to boost their child's self-esteem rather than to diminish it by winning themselves.

• When children lose, it can be as if the bottom of their world has fallen out, as if they have been destroyed.

Parents can help their children learn to come to terms with the despair of losing by letting them lose *occasionally* in their games with you. Plan for such a defeat for your children; give them, say, ten minutes (but it could be as long as you have time and energy for) to express the words and tears of despair that accompany losing. In their anger and upset, they may hit or kick out at you. You can contain their blows while letting them know that you will listen to their disappointment *and* you won't let them hurt you. They need to cry out the tears of anger and despair, but they don't need to hurt you – that will only make them feel bad about themselves.

Children need both to experience the joy of being the champion and to have the chance to scream out the despair of losing. This will help them towards becoming at ease with both winning and losing, not only with you but also when they compete with other children.

BOYS' ATTITUDES TO GIRLS AND WOMEN (AND THEMSELVES)

'GIRLS. YUK!'

A boy learns to define himself as a boy in contrast to girls (see Understanding Masculinity, page 122). A boy can be whatever a girl is not. Boys will often exclude girls from their games, or may want only tomboys – girls who act like boys – to join in with them. One of the ways in which boys separate themselves off from girls is by putting them down: 'We don't play with girls', 'Boys are better than girls' or 'Girls. Yuk!' are the kinds of things that boys may say about girls.

But boys' attitudes to girls also affect the way they – boys – behave. If a boy behaves in non-macho and traditionally feminine ways, he may be put down by other boys (and girls) for not being properly masculine. Terms of abuse may be 'sissy' or 'gay', the ultimate derogatory term of abuse towards a boy with its connotation that he is not a 'real man'. The fear of being labelled gay keeps boys and men acting the tough male, when underneath they may not feel themselves to be that kind of man at all.

So there is an intimate connection between boys needing to learn to respect both themselves and females, because if boys can learn to respect girls and women, then they must also learn to respect themselves, and vice versa.

RAISING BOYS' SELF-ESTEEM

'I sometimes think about the things people say about boys. "They're a pain." "They're so much more trouble." "You always have to tell them off about something." "Girls are so much easier." And I wonder what it must be like for boys to live in a society where there are so many negative things being said about them.' Patricia

It's hard to feel good about yourself if all around you critical comments are being made, even if they are about your gender rather than about you as an individual. And for a boy to have a positive sense of self-esteem, he needs to know that other people like him. Thus, it is important to appreciate boys both for who they are and for what they do; not only so that they can grow into self-respecting men but also so they can learn to respect girls and women. You need to respect yourself before you can respect others.

You may think it sounds easy to appreciate people, but in our (British) society we tend not to say positive things about each other. We seem to fear that if we appreciate other people they will become boastful and too big for their boots, and that they might start blowing their own trumpets rather than being modest about themselves. Many people feel embarrassed both when appreciating others (including their children) and when being appreciated. Rather than feel the embarrassment, we just don't appreciate.

Parents, too, are often in the habit of pointing out their children's mistakes, with the positive intention of helping them learn from those mistakes. But being repeatedly told that you are doing things wrong is demoralising, while being told what you are doing well is uplifting and encouraging.

'I can remember my parents constantly telling me what I was doing wrong. I don't ever remember them telling me what I was doing well. Thus, I've been spurred on to make an effort to appreciate my children . . . but it has not been easy!

'I found "helpful" criticisms coming out of my mouth – "You haven't wiped the table properly" and "You've left your socks lying on the floor" – which were said with the intention of helping the children learn to do their jobs

properly in future. I had to work hard to think of the positive statements – "Thank you for wiping the table" and "It makes a real difference to me when you put your dirty clothes in the washing basket" – and to assume that they would get better at their jobs with practice.

'I think they prefer my appreciations. They do seem to glow and I think we get better results. And in addition I feel better in myself. I used to feel that I was always nagging them, whereas now I just enjoy telling them positive things."
Della

Learning to appreciate your sons, telling them what you like about them and what you like about what they do will play its part in helping them learn to feel good about themselves and who they are.

RESPECTING GIRLS
For much of their childhood, until puberty, boys and girls tend to play in separate sex groups. Many of the comments between them, particularly from boys to girls, consist of name-calling and derogatory comments. What can parents (and others) do to encourage boys to be respectful in their attitudes and behaviour towards girls?

They can intervene in situations where boys are putting down a girl, as in the following example from Maureen.

'Robin and Brian, his cousin, were playing together in the garden when Hannah came out to play with them. They started teasing her and calling her names. I heard them doing this and, because I don't like the way boys often put down

girls, I intervened and said I didn't want them to talk to
Hannah like that.

'They were rather sheepish about being told off, but we
had a good talk when I asked them how they would feel if they
were a girl and if two boys ganged up on them.' Maureen

Maureen's intervention had two goals: the first was to
stop the boys putting down the girl (so that the boys
and the girl were clear that Maureen did not approve of
what was happening) and the second was to educate
the boys by initiating a conversation with them to help
them understand what it was like to be the target of
teasing and name-calling. The aim of this would be to
make them less likely to participate in such behaviour
on future occasions, whether directed at girls or any
other group of people.

'DON'T TALK TO YOUR MOTHER LIKE THAT'

'When John's friends come round and I ask them to do
something, they never listen to me. But if Peter asks them,
they respond straight away. And it's the same with John. He
hardly ever listens to me, though if his dad speaks to him he
is much more likely to do what he is told. I think it's pure
sexism.' Patricia

If you are a mother reading this, you may recognise the
way in which boys are often more prepared to listen to
their fathers, or other men, than to their mothers, or
other women.

When a boy takes notice only of his father and does
not listen to his mother, it can be particularly helpful if

someone (ideally the father, but it could in practice be anybody) points this out to him and talks with him about getting him to recognise and then change his behaviour. A mother can, of course, speak up for herself, but the word of another person is more likely to be heard by the boy.

'Backchat' from boys to their mothers often becomes a particular problem when boys are approaching puberty. At this point in their lives boys may start to act big, flex their muscles and try to show their mother who's the boss.

The point at which a boy starts talking back to his mother is the point at which she needs someone to say to him, 'Don't talk to you mother like that' so that he does not continue to talk to her in that way. If the intervention comes from another woman, the boy could easily reject the content of what is being said to him and instead to say to himself: 'These women. They're always complaining.' An intervention from a man will not elicit the same response and is, in fact, more likely to be listened to and acted on.

If a boy treats his mother disrespectfully, whether by ignoring her or by being rude to her, his behaviour needs to be stopped, for both their sakes. It hurts a boy to be allowed to be disrespectful towards his mother, whether physically or verbally, just as it hurts her.

SEXUALITY

'My parents never talked with me about the facts of life; they were much too embarrassed. When I was 11 years old my mother gave me a pamphlet to read about the facts of life. It

talked about how the boy had to put his seed into the girl in order to make a baby. I was very naive in those days, and it just left me with a picture of a flower growing in a pot.'
Paul

Sex and sexuality are much more in the public domain today than they were in the past. Sexual relationships (often the sexual misdemeanours of prominent people) are discussed openly in public, they are in the news, on television and in newspapers. It is almost impossible for parents to 'protect' their children's innocence and keep them from learning about things that parents may consider to be more appropriate for when they are older.

Where possible, it is helpful if both parents talk with their sons (and daughters) about sex and sexuality at the appropriate time (see below), rather than delegating the subject to one parent.

Even though we live at a time of apparent openness about sexuality, many parents still feel embarrassed discussing and answering their children's questions on sexuality. However parents have an important role to play, even though sex education is on the curriculum at school.

Parents can use the following ideas to discuss sex and sexuality with boys.

• When boys first learn about sex and rude words, they may snigger and giggle about what they have learned, and repeat their 'naughty' words over and over again. This is a normal phase that many boys go through. An angry reaction on your part may tend to make boys continue doing the very things they have discovered make you angry, exercising their new-found power over you. Instead, you could try ignoring this behaviour or responding to it in a light and humorous way. You may want to talk with your son about the fact that other people may not like his behaviour and may react angrily to it, and so set boundaries with him as to where and when he says his 'naughty' words.

• Different families have a whole spectrum of attitudes towards sexuality. Take, for example, the issues of parents' nudity in front of their children. Some families are comfortable about being naked in front of their children while others are not. There is no one right way to be. What is important is for family members to respect each other's wishes. When a boy reaches puberty he may no longer want his mother coming into the bathroom or his bedroom when he is in a state of undress. The closed door of the bathroom or bedroom helps to keep open the door of the relationship between a boy and his parents.

• Talk about and acknowledge sexual matters when they arise in the course of normal events, rather than saving them for particular times and situations. For example, if you are in the bathroom at the same time as your son, he may make comments about his body or yours. Or if you are watching television and a sexual matter is portrayed – which, of course, happens in programmes as varied as soaps or the news – take the opportunity to initiate a conversation about what you have seen or heard, or answer as honestly as possible any questions that your son (or daughter) may pose. Try to respond to his comments and questions as honestly as possible.

• You may feel embarrassed about talking about sex with your son (or daughter). Acknowledge your embarrassment to them rather than pretending that you are not embarrassed – they will sense your embarrassment anyway.

• As puberty approaches, boys will have their first wet dreams and develop an interest in masturbation. This is completely normal. It may bring strong feelings in you, perhaps of disapproval or of a sense that 'my little boy has lost his innocence'. However, try to remember that he needs people around him who can support him and help him understand these new and powerful emotions that he is feeling. He may be starting to feel sexual attraction towards girls and women which may come as a shock when, for a number of years, he has mainly wanted to be in the company of boys.

Your son may not feel able to talk to you about his sexual feelings. In this case you may need to find an adult friend whose opinions you value to whom he can talk. He needs some adult guidance to prevent him from falling under the misguided influence of his peers – or others – who themselves may be poorly informed and have little or no guidance.

PORNOGRAPHY

Pornography can particularly be an issue for boys – and their parents. Boys may be interested in furtively looking at pornographic magazines which they see daily on the top shelf; they may have discovered hard-core pornography on computer disks in the school playground or on the Internet, and they may have seen similar material on cable or satellite television channels. They may feel too embarrassed to talk about any knowledge they may have of, or interest in, pornography with their parents, and their parents may be most embarrassed to talk about it to them. How should parents respond to their sons' interest in pornography?

• A passing interest in pornography among boys who are entering puberty is normal. If parents can respond to it as such, then boys are likely to move on from their interest in pornography to wanting to start to explore their sexuality and to form intimate relationships as they grow into young adulthood. You may choose to acknowledge and accept your son's interest, but if you overreact by, for example, telling him off in no uncertain terms or banning pornographic literature from the house, then he may well feel pushed into an even greater interest in – and use of – pornography.

Alternatively, you could try to engage in a discussion with your son about pornography – both to listen to his views and to share your own opinions. You may want to talk with him about how much advertising uses women's bodies to sell products or how pornography turns women into sex objects. After such a discussion, you can decide with your son how to deal with the issue of pornography in your family –

whether he can have pornographic magazines or videos in the house.

• What do you do if your son wants to put up pictures of naked women in his room and you do not approve? At first glance there seems to be a simple choice of allowing him to do what he wants (because it is *his* room) or telling him that you will not permit such pictures in *your* house. But perhaps the most important thing is to have a discussion with him and to ask him questions such as: 'Why do you want those pictures on your wall?', 'What do they mean to you?' and 'How do you think your mother (and sister or younger brother) will feel about them?' Having had the discussion with your son you can, of course, decide whether to let him make his own decision, whether to negotiate some sort of compromise or whether to impose your wishes.

Mothers may find particular difficulty in having these conversations with their sons and, especially if you are a mother bringing up your son on your own, you may find it helpful to turn to a trusted adult male friend to help you talk about these issues with your son.

• Many of us have strong views about pornography. We may well have fixed views about the porn industry, about whether we are attracted to pornography, how we feel about using (or not using) it, and how we feel about other people using it. However, parents may not have thought about the issue of their sons being interested in pornography before actually discovering that they are. Rather than reacting spontaneously, and in a way that they might later regret, parents could take some time to explore their own feelings, to listen to other parents talking about their sons and pornography, and to working out their views and how they would like to respond. A thought-out response in situations where we have strong feelings is always better than a knee-jerk reaction to a new and difficult situation.

LACK OF INTEREST IN SCHOOL

The introduction to this book highlighted the fact that some boys are now underachieving in schools, even in traditionally 'male' subjects. A number of reasons, starting from the earliest years in children's lives, have been put forward for this.

GIRLS' EARLY ADVANTAGES

• Girls mature more quickly than boys and are readier to start learning at an earlier age.
• Girls' verbal skills mean that generally they start to talk, read and write earlier than boys.
• Talking plays a central part in the way girls relate to other children and adults, which enables them to continue to develop their talking skills, while boys tend to immerse themselves more in activities and to talk less, thus exacerbating their slower development of language.
• Children are more likely to be read to at home by their mothers, which, from early on, gives them an image of reading as a female activity.
• Girls have been described as having 'on-the-table

skills'. They involve themselves easily in intricate table-top activities, whereas boys prefer to sit or lie on the floor and play with larger construction toys.

• Girls have a greater span of concentration, which helps them persevere with tasks that they may not be able to perform at the first attempt, whereas boys are more likely to cruise from one activity to another, as each one holds their attention for only a limited period of time, and they then give up on an activity when they cannot immediately solve a problem.

• Girls' verbal skills are valued by the education system more than the spatial skills of boys. As a result, girls' self-esteem is boosted, while boys are told off for messing around and misbehaving or not being so successful at their work.

• The majority of teachers in primary schools are women, so they give the impression that teaching and learning are 'female' activities.

Thus, girls' early educational advantages are confirmed and extended by what happens at home and school.

BOYS IN PRIMARY SCHOOL

Boys' conditioning plays its part in holding them back as they assert themselves in the classroom.

• Boys are more likely to distinguish themselves from the girls, who apply themselves to their work, by messing around and being noisy and jokey.

• Boys do not like to fail, or be seen to fail, so they are more likely to opt out of learning than to face challenges at which they might not succeed.

- Boys see themselves as risk-takers who like to be involved in action and excitement rather than having to face what they see as the tedium of reading and writing.
- Boys tend to be competitive and individualistic and are not very good at cooperating when working in groups.

As a result, some teachers confront boys' eagerness, misbehaviour and desire for action with reprimands, which leads boys to hold even stronger anti-learning attitudes. And boys often enjoy the attention they get when they are told off and sent out of the classroom, feeling that their status is enhanced through such challenging of authority. Teachers, as can be imagined, may find girls easier to teach because of what has been described as their passive learning style.

In these circumstances it is easy for teachers to label boys even before they have had them in their class.

'My daughter, Sheena, was in Mrs B's class at primary school in Year 2. She did very good work in the class. She was liked by Mrs B, and Sheena liked her teacher, too.

'Two years later her younger brother, Bruno, came into Mrs B's Year 2 class. Early in the year we met Mrs B at a social event and, perhaps in an unguarded moment, she said: "Sheena did very well when she was with me, but I don't expect Bruno to do so well – he's a boy, and you can't expect so much from them." ' Lesley

As already discussed, labelling is dangerous, because very often labels are self-fulfilling. It is well recognised that at school a child will perform to a teacher's expectations. If a teacher thinks a child is bright, then he or she is more likely to perform well than if the teacher thinks he or she is a slow learner.

BOYS IN SECONDARY SCHOOL

The early advantages that girls show in learning are continued throughout their schooling. In the past, boys caught up with girls and overtook them by the end of their schooling, but this no longer happens (see Some Statistics, page 10). With the changes in the job market, which have meant that there are fewer traditionally male jobs, boys can no longer be sure of getting a permanent job at the end of their education, and this, along with the factors of gender conditioning, plays its part in demotivating them from applying themselves to their work at school.

MAKING SCHOOLS AND BOYS FIT

There is talk of 'the feminisation of the classroom' so that now boys are being disadvantaged. As a consequence, changes in the way of teaching need to be introduced, without turning the clock back so that girls are again disadvantaged, but which find ways of boosting boys' learning.

A number of ideas are being tried in schools to encourage boys' interest in learning, ranging from encouraging more men to teach in primary schools, attracting boys' interest by making media such as computers and CD-ROMs available, teaching boys and girls in separate sex groups at GCSE, and reintroducing more competitive testing in which boys appear to shine.

HOW PARENTS CAN SUSTAIN THEIR BOYS' INTEREST IN LEARNING

• One of the main concerns with boys is their lack of interest in books and reading, which they may see as 'female'. If a boy has contact with his father, it is useful if he can read with him. And if he does not have contact with his father, then it can be useful for him to have contact with one or more adult male friends who can read with and act as 'mentors' to him.

• Another possible reason why boys often do not read books is because many of the books available – mostly fiction – may not appeal to their particular interests; boys are often more interested in non-fiction.

• Ensure that you have fun reading books together, rather than allowing reading to become a dry, educational venture. Some parents play around with reading, where they read one line or paragraph and their sons read the next, or they even alternate words from time to time. As long as you are both having fun, your sons are likely to gain interest in books and learn, rather than being put off.

• Some boys simply do not like reading books. However, books are not the only medium for reading, as shown in the following story:

'John would never read a book, and we were concerned about his reading level, but, on talking to his class teacher, were reassured to hear that his reading was fine. We think he must be broadening his vocabulary from the instructions that he sees on the computer screen and the words that he

reads in his sticker albums. He certainly doesn't read books at home!' Patricia

- Boys tend not to have as broad a vocabulary as girls, which also disadvantages them in school. Thus, it can be particularly helpful for them if parents talk with them and encourage them to discuss a variety of topics. An obvious place to start is with what interests them rather than with subjects that appear to be particularly educational. The more talking and listening you can introduce into your relationship with your sons, the more likely it is to help them at school.
- Computers and computer games have a special appeal to boys. Although the content of much of what they play may not be educational, there are on-screen instructions that have to be read, and skills in dexterity that can be developed.
- Much time may be spent in front of the television. Although many of the programmes that attract boys have little educational content, parents who sit down and watch with their sons (and daughters) can talk with them about what they have seen and ask for their views about it.
- Boys tend to be slapdash with their homework, spending as little time over it as possible, in contrast to girls, who like to ensure that they have completed their task adequately. Parents can be of great help to their sons by supervising their homework and ensuring that they do it to the best of their ability.
- If your sons are doing homework at home, ensure that they work in short bursts and get to take enough breaks to let off excess energy.

- If you are concerned about your son's lack of interest in reading or lack of application to his work, you may like to talk to his teacher. There is a growing awareness in schools and among teachers of the difficulties boys face and a desire to develop strategies to help them.

You cannot turn your sons into geniuses, but you can help them learn to apply themselves to their work.

THE WIMP

In this chapter we have discussed a number of aspects of boys' behaviour that many parents find difficult. However, the idea that boys will be boys, and the types of behaviour identified, are part and parcel of what we expect when bringing up boys. If boys do not fit this mould – and the difficulties it brings with it – then we may have another set of concerns: that boys are not 'manly' enough, that they may not fit in, that they may become the target of other people's jokes and be seen as wimps.

'Junior's such a lovely boy. He's thoughtful, he treats people well, and he has a broad range of interests. He likes reading, he plays the piano, and he is very good at taking care of the pets, a dog and a cat. In fact, he is everything I could wish for in a son.

'However, I'm concerned for him because he doesn't share the same interests as most other boys. He doesn't have many friends, and he seems to be rather an outsider. He's not "one of the lads" – not that I really want him to be. I don't think

the others make fun of him, but I'm worried that might happen too.' Charmaine

SUPPORTING BOYS IN THEIR FRIENDSHIPS

There are a limited number of passports into boys' culture which enable boys to befriend one another. Sport is one, as are games that involve fighting and shooting with guns. What adults often forget is that the activity is important because it is the *means* by which boys make contact with each other. The actual content of the activity, however, may not have much significance in itself.

A boy who is naturally skilled at football is likely to feel part of the in-crowd and to be admired by other boys. Some boys learn lots of facts about professional football clubs and players – even though they are not at all interested in the subject – because they realise that this is a way in which they can make friends with other boys. Once a boy has made contact with another, the two of them may find another, different interest in common.

Perhaps you have brought up your son to avoid games that involve fighting and guns – but if all the boys around him are playing these games, then he has little hope of making friends unless he can join in with them. He may not, of course, be particularly interested in fighting games. Once he has been accepted as one of the gang, however, he has more chance of finding a friend who might share some of his other interests. Being able to 'play the dominant culture' can help boys to find their niche.

This may, of course, cause some conflict for you if

you are anti-guns. However, it is certainly possible to allow your sons to play with guns – and even to join him in gun fights – while also letting him know your views. The more you can do this in a light and relaxed way, the less likely he is to become obsessed by playing with guns, and the more likely he is just to use such games as a means of making contact with other boys.

The challenge for parents is to bring up boys who have the qualities that they want while also helping boys manage the outside world that expects them to fit into a particular rigid mould. And life can get difficult for boys who do not fit that mould. Thus, it is important to recognise that boys can exhibit both traditionally male characteristics as well as traditionally female ones.

Chapter Four

WHY PARENTS FIND THESE SOLUTIONS DIFFICULT AND WHAT THEY CAN DO

Parents often find the solutions suggested in the last chapter difficult to implement. Why is this?

RELATIONSHIP WITH YOUR OWN PARENTS

Your experience of being parented is the key factor that influences how you relate to your children. Parents tend to repeat with their own children the patterns of behaviour that they learned at *their* parents' knees. As a result, parents who were repeatedly criticised are likely to be critical of their children, and parents who grew up with warmth and affection are likely to bring up their children in a home full of warmth and affection.

SAME AND OPPOSITE PARENTING
A concept that is useful in describing parenting down the generations is 'same' and 'opposite' parenting. 'Same' parents are parents who repeat the patterns of behaviour of their own parents with their children, perhaps because they had a mainly happy childhood and want to give their children a similar experience.

Some parents who were unhappy as children try to be 'opposite' parents, doing the opposite of what their parents did in order to give their children a different experience. 'Opposite' parents may on the surface treat their children differently from how they were treated, but they tend unwittingly to pass on the same underlying patterns of behaviour, as shown in the following story.

'My parents criticised me a great deal when I was a child, and I vowed to be different with my children. I repeatedly praised Jimmy when he was growing up and told him how much I loved him. But now he is eleven I have found out from his teachers that he will only do his work when they tell him how well he is doing. It's as if he's dependent on the praise from the outside because, like me, he doesn't know on the inside that he is all right. It has been very painful to realise this, when it had been my "mission" to change the way I brought up my children from the way I had been brought up.' Sarah

It can be difficult to break out of the patterns of parenting that we experienced as children. Even though Sarah tried hard to be different from her parents, she was unaware that what she was passing on to her son was her own low self-esteem. It was not enough just to replace the criticisms she had received with praise and appreciation. She actually needed to find a way to boost her own self-esteem. If she could find a way to feel more confident in herself, then she would be able to model to Jimmy how he could feel more confident in himself.

GENDER-ROLE EXPECTATIONS

Another factor that influences parents is the gender expectations that their parents had of them as children. If you grew up in a family in which there were clear expectations about how boys and girls should behave, then these gender expectations may affect the expectations you have for your children – even if you try to go against them.

Society's expectations of what boys and girls can and should do are changing, as are parents' expectations for their sons and daughters. But parents can not change their own behaviour overnight, and they may find themselves behaving in 'old' ways that they have perhaps taken on from their childhood, when in fact they would rather behave in 'new' ways.

'I can remember my brother and I arguing non-stop with our parents. We said that they treated us differently because of our genders, but they said it had nothing to do with gender – or anything else. They said they treated us differently because we were different.

'Looking back, however, I think we reflected two generations living in changing times. My parents grew up with traditional gender-role expectations – the man goes out to work, the woman stays at home – and those were incontrovertible facts to them. Their expectations for us were in line with what they thought men and women and boys and girls should do. But we were part of the generation that rejected all that and believed that girls could do anything boys could do.

'As a parent now, however, I have more understanding of

my parents. I realise that old ways die hard, and I sometimes find that the thoughts in my mind are different from the intentions that I would like to have.' Sarah

Take a few minutes to reflect on your own childhood and the ways in which your parents related to you. With the benefit of hindsight, how much do you think their expectations of you were affected by your gender? This may be easier to think about if you had a sibling of the opposite sex, because then you can compare directly how your parents treated you with how they treated your brother or sister.

Notice the ways in which you still feel bound by any gender expectations that your parents had of you. It is all too easy to take on the expectations of your parents and make them your own – whether you actually want to or not. You may 'internalise' some of those expectations so that you believe, for example, that mothers are better at caring for their children than fathers, or that a father's role is to discipline his children and it is for a mother to be close and intimate with them.

'I can still hear the phrase "Wait till your father gets home" ringing in my ears. I reject it now and believe that mothers need to discipline their children as much as fathers do, just as fathers need to be close to their children like mothers.

'But I do find it hard to be firm with the children. I have this image in my head that it's Ian's role to discipline the children and lay down the law, even though the reality is clearly different – the children are so excited to see Ian when

he gets home that they jump on him rather than holding back fearfully.' Christine

You may not want to act in accordance with those 'inherited' values with your children, but if those values are what you believe deep down, then it is likely that they will play a part in affecting how you relate to your sons and daughters.

CHANGING EXPECTATIONS
It is an act of great courage to dare to reflect on your own behaviour and to notice some of the ways in which you would like to change. And the first step in changing your behaviour is to become aware of some of the values that guide your actions – values that you may not have chosen.

'I had been conscious that Jordan was always demanding my attention and needing help, whereas Geraldine just got on with things. When I thought some more about it, I was reminded of my childhood and how things had been similar between my brother and me: I just got on with things on my own, whereas he always seemed to need – and get – someone to be with him.

'I didn't like seeing this aspect of my relationship with my brother in my own children. At first it upset me greatly, and I turned to friends for support with the way I felt. After a while I realised that it was better to notice it – however painful that was – than not. At least that gave me the chance to do something about it. And I hit on a strategy of requiring Jordan to do things on his own and offering to do things with Geraldine.

'At least we are starting to change the balance of relationships in the family. Though it is hard work.'
Margaret

Changing patterns of thought and belief that have governed your life for many years is likely to require a determined effort on your part. And such changes take time.

A NEW FAMILY DANCE

Relationships are like a dance. Each member of the family will be dancing in step, whether it is a harmonious dance or a conflictual dance. If you want to change the way people relate within the family, one way of doing so is through changing your own dance. However, other family members are unlikely to want to take up your new dance without much resistance and attempts to get you back into the dance they all know and feel safe with. But a new dance opens up all kinds of possibilities. And changing your own steps in the family dance is more likely to bring about change in the family than if you just act to try to change the steps of other family members.

'I gradually realised that I was being a martyr-mother – always saying "yes" to the children, unless there was a good reason for saying "no". So I decided to try to be a mother who looked after her own needs as well as the children's.

'One thing I didn't like doing was dressing Harry, who was five, and I knew he was quite capable of dressing himself. So I set my weekend strategy and met an hour and a half of tears and tantrums on Saturday morning with a resolve not

to give in and dress him. He did – cleverly – exchange the T-shirt I gave him for one with buttons, which I did up because I knew he couldn't.

'My next big test was on Monday morning, and I resolved to take him to school, dressed or not. He must have known I meant business, because my time warnings were enough for him to get himself dressed.

'But the biggest surprise was when Sally, my seven-year-old daughter, said, "Mum, will you dress me?" on Sunday, the second day that Harry had to dress himself. My actions of refusing to be a martyr-mother and sticking up for myself had reverberations around the family – I created space for my daughter to be able to ask for what she wanted.' Alex

Alex realised that she was dancing to the martyr-step. As she put her attention on changing her step, she enabled Sally to create a new step for herself, without intending to do so. Margaret (in the previous example) experienced trying to change the relationship between Jordan and Geraldine as 'hard', whereas Alex's experience led to unexpected and almost immediate changes from Sally. New steps from the dancer – that is, modelling new behaviour – are more likely to lead to change than trying to teach others new steps.

FATHERS AND SONS

Parents are so close to their children that it can be hard for them to know where they end and where their children begin. The joke about the mother who says to her child 'I'm cold. Put your coat on' is a good illustration of this. When parents feel something, it is all too easy for them to assume that their children feel the same thing, rather than checking out with them what they actually feel.

The task for many parents is to disentangle their own feelings from their children's. How, in particular, does this relate to fathers and sons?

LIVING YOUR DREAMS THROUGH YOUR SON

Many adults had dreams when they were young which they may not have been able to live out, for whatever reason. Perhaps, for example, you wanted to achieve a certain goal but did not have the ability or the opportunity, or perhaps your dream was not valued and encouraged by the family you grew up in. Whatever the circumstances, if you were unable to fulfil your dream, you may unconsciously transfer the hope that your child can live out your dream for you. This is discussed under the heading Fathers and Sons, because it is more likely to happen between a parent and a same-sex child, though this is something for both parents to be aware of.

'Like many small boys, when I was young I wanted to be a footballer. I was good enough to play for the school, though I don't think I really had the ability to get any further. But nobody in my family shared my dream with me, and I was left with the feeling "if only."

'I've played lots of football with Gregory, my son, and encouraged him a lot. I'm sure that's played a significant part in helping him to be so good at football. Now he has dreams of being a star and, while I want to encourage him, I'm concerned that I don't burden him with my dreams for him.

*'Gregory knows about my dreams, and I have made it
clear to him that he must make his own decisions as to how
far he wants to take his football, but I'm concerned that he
may be scared of disappointing me.'* Chris

Chris was left with the dull ache of a dream that he
could not let go of. It was all too easy for his own dream
to be revived by his son, particularly as his son had
talents in the same arena. Chris may have got his
dream out of his system if he had had the chance to
really go for it as a child, whether he had achieved it or
not, or if he had been encouraged to express his
disappointment at not being able to follow his dream,
with adults who acknowledged his feelings and
understood how important the dream had been for
him.

Boys (and girls) need encouragement in their
dreams. They need to be able to create visions of what
they want for themselves and to know that they can
aspire to them. There may be disappointments if they
aren't able to fulfil their dreams, but they need to be
helped to face these. If they are discouraged from
dreaming in order to protect them from possible
disappointment, then they will learn that life is about
settling for what you can get, not going for what you
really want. And what is important is that they learn
that they can 'go for it'.

Fathers need to ensure that any of their leftover
dreams do not interfere in their relationship with their
sons (and daughters). The best a father can do for his
son is to encourage him to go for what he wants and to
try to put aside what he, the father, might want for his

son. But if he finds difficulty in putting his feelings to one side, then he can be open with his son, so that his son does not feel manipulated by his father's unexpressed feelings. If father and son can talk together, this will make it more likely that the son will be able to decide what he wants to do in his own life, rather than feeling that he has to live out his life to please his father.

CLOSENESS BETWEEN FATHER AND SON

'I did feel close to my father, and I think he felt close to me, but I never really knew where I stood with him until he was on his deathbed.

'It was only then that he was able to tell me what a good son I had been and how proud he was of me. And he even said, "I love you," those words I hadn't heard since I had been a small boy. I'm so glad we shared that time together before he died, but I do so wish that expression of feeling could have played a bigger part in our lives.' Geoff

Traditionally, fathers and sons (like men in general) do not share their feelings. They are unlikely to express warmth and affection together; hugging and kissing are likely to stop at a boy's early age; and father and son rarely talk about their fears and concerns with one another.

A father and son may feel close with one another, but it is more likely to be expressed by a slap on the back or the sharing of an activity than to be expressed openly in words and actions. If fathers and sons feel close, it is likely to be closeness at a distance.

These patterns of behaviour can be difficult to change. A father may want to be physically and emotionally close to his son, but he may not have the wherewithal within him to be that kind of man. Fathers need to learn to appreciate and accept themselves for the way they are with their children, and they also need appreciation and acceptance from their partners. Women can get impatient with men for being unable to let down the barriers that prevent them from openly expressing their feelings. But patience and acceptance rather than a 'full-frontal assault' may enable them to change and openly express and receive affection.

COMPETITIVENESS AND ISOLATION

'When I was a child my father always knew everything best. If we did homework together, he was always pointing out my mistakes – so that I would avoid them in future. If we played a game together, he would always win – to spur me on to greater things next time. So I learned that a father had to be strong and competent.

'I'm embarrassed to say that I used to think that I had to be like that with my son. I showed off and impressed him with everything that I did – in order to make a big, strong man out of him, too.

'At the time I didn't realise that he needed warmth and appreciation from me as well as a strong and confident role model. Now I'm trying to share both sides of myself. But it's not easy, when I only have my father as an example.' Henry

If a man grew up having to compete with his father, this competitiveness may also be played out in his relationship with his sons. As Henry says, his only experience was how his father was with him, so he had no other example. Along with the competitiveness goes a sense of isolation. A father who competes with his sons has to hold himself apart, because he cannot let himself be close to a rival. But this is not what many men want in their relationships with their sons today. Acknowledging the competitiveness and rivalry, possibly talking about it with your sons and then behaving differently, can all help to break down this separation.

MOTHERS AND SONS

'I was an only child so had no experience of growing up with boys. When I had my boys, it was a completely new experience for me. Not from when they were born, because at first they were just babies, no different from Sonya, my daughter.

'Differences only really showed themselves when they started mixing with other boys. Then it was the relentlessness of their fighting and the endless giggling about rude words and bodily functions (such as farting and burping) that annoyed me the most.

'I couldn't understand why they had to fight and hurt each other, nor could I understand what they saw in all those silly words and behaviours.

'It's also on an intuitive level. I feel in tune with Sonya. I feel I understand her and know what makes her tick. But I don't feel that with the boys. They sometimes seem like such strange alien beings.' Melanie

A boy may be a completely new entity to a mother, particularly if she did not grow up with brothers. A mother may become especially conscious of her son's gender when he starts to interact with others in the outside world. As Melanie says, a mother may not be able to understand how her son thinks, feels and behaves, which may contrast with a more intuitive connection that she has with her daughter, because she feels she is able to understand her from the inside.

RELATIONSHIP WITH HER OWN FATHER

Mothers' attitudes towards their sons are likely to be shaped by their own experiences with their fathers in just the same way that fathers' attitudes towards their sons are likely to be shaped by theirs. A mother who had a warm and loving relationship with her father is likely to feel warm and loving towards her son.

'My father had lots of time for me. He was always pleased to see me, he played with me when he was around, and he even seemed reasonable when he told me off.

'I now feel really warmly towards my boys, and I feel that I have lots of time and patience with them, just as he had for me.

'Friends find their boys' aggression and noisiness difficult. But I actually like those qualities. Although my father wasn't like that, the "maleness" of their behaviour reminds me of him.' Alex

Because 'maleness', through her father, played a part in building Alex's self-esteem, it holds positive associations for her. Her sons' maleness also holds positive associations for her, and she is able to reflect a positive sense to her sons that is likely to help them feel good about being male.

However, a positive feeling towards your father is not a guarantee of a positive relationship with and feelings towards your sons.

'I loved my father very much and really looked forward to having a son. When Jeremy was born I was very happy, and we had an easy relationship for the first few years. But after he started mixing with other boys at school, he started behaving in ways I didn't like. Was this the boy I had brought into the world? I thought to myself. Where had I gone wrong?

'I had, perhaps simplistically, expected a simple repetition of my relationship with my father. But I ended up with a son behaving in ways that I actually could not stand.' Jude

Both Alex's and Jude's stories are similar, but one ends up feeling very differently about her son than the other. Could it just be chance, or would psychology offer an opinion – that in Jude's case, perhaps she had an idealistic view of her father which led her to have an idealistic view of her son? And so she was a demanding mother – rather than an accepting mother, as was Alex – who became angry and disappointed when her son did not live up to her ideals.

In a similar fashion, a mother who had an unsatisfactory relationship with her father may not necessarily have a poor relationship with her sons.

What is important is for boys (and girls) to have the

feeling of being accepted for who they are. This may come easily for some mothers, but others will have to work at it more.

A BOY SEPARATING FROM HIS MOTHER

A girl, on realising her femaleness, grows if anything closer to her mother. For a boy, growing up means becoming less like his mother. How his mother handles this separation is important, especially in a world in which men play only a small part in childcare. If men were around them, boys would embark on a process of becoming more like their fathers.

A boy needs his mother to understand that his new ways of behaving are not a rejection of her but his attempts to work out what a man is. He may take up a macho stance, and his mother may choose to help him understand that there are other ways of being a man, and this is fine. What will hurt is to give him the feeling that there is something wrong with him for being male. A boy needs to know that his maleness is good and to be guided, if necessary, in his exploration.

'Gregory got into a phase of hitting, shortly after he started school. I think he thought it was the masculine way to get things. And, thinking about the programmes he watched on children's TV, I can see why he thought that.

'I worked hard with his teachers, letting him know that it was fine to want things but that life is not a TV series, and in life we "say it with words and not with punches." It took a while, but it sank in. Thankfully, the hitting has virtually stopped.' Jennifer

Boys often behave in ways that mothers may find difficult. Again, a mother needs to try to be accepting of her sons, while either finding a new way to view the behaviour or rejecting the behaviour while accepting her son.

PHYSICAL GAMES

'Sometimes Gregory gives Chris a mock punch in the stomach when Chris comes home in the evenings. I don't like it at all, but Chris just picks Gregory up, gives him a hug and laughs.

'Or there are other times when they play fighting games. I'm always worrying that somebody will get hurt. But they just think I'm being a spoilsport and tell me to leave them alone.

'But then, if Gregory tries these things with me, I just get angry. I don't consider them fun, and I don't want him doing them with me.' Jennifer

There's something in the physical relationship between fathers and sons which often does not play a part in the relationship between mothers and sons. Few mothers choose to integrate these ways of being into their relationships with their sons. Sons do not need their mothers to behave the same as their fathers, but what will help them is for their mothers to accept that this is the way they like to behave with their fathers and that there is nothing wrong with it.

A mother who cannot accept this may find her son drawing away from her.

FIGHTING

Most boys like to fight; most girls do not. Women often express the fear that if their sons fight, then they may turn into violent men. However, the reverse is if anything true. Boys whose aggression is suppressed are more likely to turn out to be violent in later years than boys who have been allowed to express aggression. Again, it is helpful if mothers can find ways of assisting their sons to channel their aggression so that nobody gets hurt rather than suppressing it so that it gets hidden away inside.

Chapter Five

LEARNING TO BE A MAN

LACK OF MALE ROLE MODELS

How does a boy learn what it means to be a man when he primarily grows up in a world of women? Most of his day-to-day care is by women – first his mother, then his playgroup or nursery teacher, and then his primary school teacher. Needless to say, we do not need to ask the opposite question – How does a girl learn what it means to be a woman? – because a girl is constantly surrounded by women who 'teach' her through their presence.

The one area where men have reversed the trend and are present where in the past they were always absent is in the delivery suite. Now, over 90 per cent of fathers attend the birth of their children – but the vast majority of them return rapidly to the world of work. Fathers may take time off work to be with their partner, the new baby and any other children in the family, but to a great extent a new father at home sees his role as supporter to his partner (which is, of course, important) rather than as an equal in caring for the baby. Right from the start, mothers are considered to be the experts, and fathers, seeing themselves as inexpert, take a back seat and disappear as quickly as they appeared.

Due to changing patterns of work and relationships,

a mother's world is more likely to consist of juggling work and home. Girls learn about all aspects of what it means to be a woman, not only because they see their mothers for so much of the time but also because their mothers are likely to talk to them about the details of their lives when away from the home. As a result, girls get a rounded picture of what it means to be a woman.

It is different when it comes to boys. Even if the father lives in the family home, he is likely to be out at work for much of the time. Men in the United Kingdom work longer hours than any of their European counterparts, they spend three times as many hours in paid work as mothers, and they work their longest hours when their children are young – to supplement an often-reduced family income while their partners either stay at home or return to work on a part-time basis. And when they come home, they may see little of their young children, who may already be in bed or, if they spend time with their children, they are more likely to get involved in a joint activity rather than to talk about the content of their day, which continues to remain a mystery to their children.

If parents have separated, in nine out of ten cases it is mothers who bring up the children and fathers who live apart. In such a situation fathers are likely to be even more shadowy figures whom their children see only in the often-pressurised circumstances of a weekend or contact visit. A well-off father may take the role of a Father Christmas figure, plying his children with treats and presents when they are with him. At the other end of the financial spectrum, a father living apart from his children may have only a low income and visits may be sparse occasions. Such a father may not have a home to which to take his children, or he may not be able to afford to take his children out. In either case there is a huge pressure on their time together, and visits may be overshadowed by the approaching time of departure.

'I love my son very much, but it is always so painful coming towards the end of a visit. It takes time to re-establish contact with him, as we only meet every fortnight. Then, by the time we are feeling at ease with each other, it's time for me to take him home to his mother.

'I cry my eyes out when he has gone. I can understand why so many men lose contact with their children when they live apart. I sometimes think that I can't bear the constant coming together and going apart again. What makes it more bearable for me is knowing how important it is for Joe that we keep in contact.' Ashok

In many children's eyes, their father is the man they see briefly at the beginning or end of the day or at weekends, if at all. Whatever he does during the time he is away mysteriously brings in much of the family income. Thus, a boy will have an idea that he will have to go out and earn money when he is a man. He is, however, unlikely to know what that actually means.

A father who is at home for much of the time – perhaps as a result of unemployment, redundancy or self-employment; it is rarely out of choice – will often take a secondary helping-out role, even if his (female) partner works as many, or more hours than he does. Men slip easily into this role when it comes to bringing up children, while women often find it hard to let go and share child-rearing with their partners.

'Before I had children I liked the idea of sharing the childcare with my partner. I had a career that was important to me, and I saw no more reason to sacrifice it than Geoff should sacrifice his.

'So we started off by working part-time and sharing looking after the children. But I was surprised how difficult I found it. Little things would niggle. On "his" days I felt he put the children to bed too late, so they were tired next morning on "my" days. Sometimes, when he cooked for the children, I felt he wasn't giving them the balanced diet they needed. And then he would play with them and do lots of things with them, but he didn't do his fair share of the jobs around the house.

'I'm sure that he was actually fine as a father, but I had an idea in my head of how I wanted things to be and I just couldn't let go – so we're reorganising the way we operate, and Geoff now works full-time and I work part-time and organise the home and the children.' Caroline

Even where mothers and fathers share in the care of their children, they often feel a pull to revert to type. Children then see their mother taking the lead in what has traditionally been 'her domain', while they see their father taking the lead in his.

WHAT ARE FATHERS FOR?

'When I think back to my childhood, I have strong feelings about my mother – both negative and positive. But when it

comes to my father, although there are memories they fade into the background. She is clearly the physical presence that I remember, not him.' Caitlin

When you think back to your childhood, what are your images of your mother and father? Many people say that they have a dominant sense of their mother, which makes sense because generally mothers bring up children. When people think back to their fathers, the word that seems to come to mind for many is 'absence'. Maybe not just physical absence – though fathers tend to be away from the home for longer than mothers – but also emotional absence. A father may be at home, but he may not be 'present' with his children: his mind may be on jobs that need doing, or he may impose himself as harsh or authoritarian and not know how to be intimate with his children.

Though the roles of men and women are changing, mothers still usually take the primary role in childcare. Does this matter? Do children need their fathers to take on a greater share in bringing them up, or do they just need their fathers to exhibit particular qualities and actions? And what of the fact that an increasing number of boys (and girls) are growing up without a father in the home? Does this matter? What are fathers for?

WHAT DO BOYS NEED FROM THEIR FATHERS?
Research into the role of fathers concludes that boys (and girls) need sensitivity, warmth and caring from their fathers – just what they need from their mothers!

Michael Lamb, one of the leading researchers into the role of fathers, quotes a developmental psychologist

118

who, describing secure attachments, says 'what each child needs is somebody who passionately cares about what happens to them'. That person is usually the child's mother. Lamb then adapts the phrase to include fathers, saying 'children feel better when there are two people who passionately care about what happens to them'. And one could go on to say that children feel better the greater the number of people who passionately care about what happens to them. So, according to this definition, the primary task of the father – and in fact of either parent – is to care passionately about what happens to his children. Boys, in particular, need to know that their fathers care for them.

'David was really looking forward to going on a five-day school trip. But as the time approached, he got nervous about going away for what seemed to him to be such a long time. I promised him that I would keep him in my mind while he was away and that I would certainly not forget him. He also wanted to take a bit of me away with him, so we imagined that he could unzip himself and put part of my spirit inside his body. I gave him a special stone of mine to put in his pocket so he could feel "me" whenever he wanted to, and he gave me a special toy for the same purpose.

'He had a lovely time, and when he came home he rushed up to me and gave me a big hug, saying: "I felt you with me while we were away."' Jonathan

An essential part of a secure attachment between parent and child is for the parent to 'hold their child in mind' when they are not there. The more a parent can hold their child in mind, the more a child will be able to hold their parent(s) in mind as well. And this is equally true for fathers as it is for mothers.

DOES A BOY NEED A FATHER?

There is no simple answer to this question because fathers' relationships with their sons are not one-dimensional. A father is not just a role model to his sons; he may also be a provider for the family and an emotional support for his partner, or a drain on the family economically and emotionally. And expectations of fathers are different at different times, so a distant, uninvolved father in the 1950s might have been seen as the norm, whereas today he would be seen as lacking in fatherly qualities.

Controversy rages over the effect on boys of growing up in a home where the father is absent. The evidence suggests that children who grow up in homes where a father is not present are more likely to suffer from mental health problems and to have difficulties at school – they may under-perform, drop out early and complete less school; they are over-represented in the statistics for delinquency and antisocial behaviour, and they have difficulty in establishing and maintaining intimate relationships in adulthood.

But rather than being evidence that the absence of a father leads to problems, these difficulties could be a result of other factors: the poverty of most lone-mother families, the emotional isolation of lone mothers and the effects of conflict with their former partners.

On the other hand Guy Corneau, in his book *Absent Fathers, Lost Sons*, discusses some of the conclusions of research into child development and suggests that boys need their fathers particularly in the first few years of their lives, and that the absence of the father during this period leads to future difficulties. However, sons of fathers who have died are the exception to this 'rule', and Corneau suggests that these widows may have positive memories of their husbands, thus talking about them a lot and giving their sons a positive image of their father which appears to compensate for his absence. This example suggests that the mother's image of the deceased or 'absent' father makes all the difference.

Whatever point of view you take on father absence, some general conclusions can be drawn:

- Boys (and girls) need secure, warm and loving relationships with their fathers *and* mothers.
- The quality of the relationship between the father and his son (or daughter) is crucial, and not solely the fact of his presence or absence.
- Where parents have separated, boys (and girls) need the parent they live with (usually the mother) to give them *a positive image of the separated parent* (usually the father). This plays a significant part in helping their sons to feel good about being male.

Mothers who bring up their children on their own may need to work that bit harder to give their sons a positive image of their fathers than mothers who live with their partners. But it cannot be stressed too much that the quality of the relationship between a boy (or a girl) and his father (or mother) is of primary importance, and not the family form in which they are living. Thus, a warm and loving separated father may be more helpful to his son than a father living in the family home who has little time and attention for his children. And a boy may be better off having little or no contact, for example, with an alcoholic or abusive father.

UNDERSTANDING MASCULINITY

As boys start to realise that they are different from girls, both in their bodies and in the ways they are supposed to behave, they start to look for role models on how to behave. With so few 'live' male role models in their day-to-day lives, they may start to feel anxious and unsure about what it means to be a man. All they may know is that being a man is not being a woman, in other words it is being 'non-female'. In the days of more distinct gender roles, it might have been relatively clear what was required of a young man, but in today's world there is great versatility in gender roles, and being 'non-female' is not enough. Boys could usefully learn that – like girls – they need a wide range of characteristics and skills, both the traditionally 'male' and the traditionally 'female' ones. And they need to know that to do so is OK.

Boys need input from the adults around them to help them understand the world and to find their own place in it, not just the stereotypical one that is assigned to them because they are male. The rest of this chapter will outline how parents can help their sons with this challenge.

BOYS NEED INFORMATION ON WHAT IT MEANS TO BE A 'REAL' MAN

Boys in the 1990s often lack clear information about what men do. They can grow up without knowing or understanding what the future may hold for them. They need you to tell them about what men are and what they can become. They need to hear that being a man includes traditional male qualities, such as strength, confidence and ambition, as well as showing vulnerability and being gentle and expressing affection and warmth.

Otherwise they may grow up to believe the messages that come at them from the outside, and they will internalise them and believe them to be true about themselves.

Passing on this information is a continuous process; a boy needs you to give him this picture of men at any opportunity when it comes up in discussion. For example:

- when he is watching a television programme about male superheroes fighting or men behaving in stereotypical ways, you can talk with him about what men are really like and how men are much more than these stereotypes;
- at times when he has stepped over the gender divide, he may need you to explain that society puts pressure on boys to behave in a particular way and that peers may shun him when he does not go along with the 'rules';

'Peter was upset when he didn't get a part in the school play. He burst into tears, and his classmates made fun of

*him and called him a sissy. He was distraught when he
came home and didn't ever want to go back to school.*

*'We talked about the rules in society which say that boys
don't cry and that boys have to act tough however they feel
inside. And we discussed what he could do. Together we
agreed that crying was OK for boys and girls and that these
rules were silly, but that for his own sake he should try to
save his tears for home.'* Geraldine

- during conversations around the table or on the
way to and from school, you can find ways to slip in
useful information about men and men's roles and
encourage him to express his views;
- you can use disparaging comments that he makes
about girls as an opportunity to give him your ideas
on the importance of boys and men respecting girls
and women;
- bedtime can be a time for reading and telling
stories about what it means to be a 'real' man.

The opportunities are endless. Just about any situation
can be used to give boys information to help them
understand themselves and the world in which they
are living.

BOYS NEED A FRAMEWORK FOR UNDERSTANDING THE WORLD

The more you can give boys a framework for
interpreting their world, the more they will be able to
understand about being a boy and growing up in a
world that has rigid expectations about what boys are
and are not supposed to do.

'I am bringing up Ben on my own. He was very upset when he started going to school because none of the boys wanted to play with him, and they called him derogatory names. I think it was because he doesn't behave the way a boy is supposed to. He doesn't like sport. Instead he prefers bird-watching, reading and just spending time with his friends. The other children just didn't seem to want to know him, and he thought, understandably, there was something wrong with him.

'It may be because he doesn't see many men around him that he hasn't learned how boys and men are expected to behave. I decided that if he wanted to get on at school, he was going to need to understand why boys behave the way they do. So we started talking about it at home. We talked about the rigid expectations on men and how that makes it hard for boys and men to be different. He understood how it was all right to be different, but sometimes you might choose to compromise in order to find some common ground with others.

'I think he's found this helpful as he tells me about new ways he has found of responding to some of the boys at school.' Rachael

It can be a great help to boys to understand that there is a dominant male culture in the world outside the home. This knowledge will help them realise that there is nothing wrong with them if they do not fit the male stereotypes, and it will give them the choice of adapting to or choosing not to participate in aspects of that culture.

THE POWER OF STEREOTYPES

One can separate the male role models that influence boys in their development into two categories: public and private. The public male role models are composed of the images presented in the media and by men in public life. The private male role models are the images that come from fathers and other men whom a boy comes across in his daily life.

Stereotypical images of what it means to be male surround us constantly.

- On the television children are presented with apparently fearless male superheroes, often accompanied by female characters who marvel at and admire them.
- There's hardly any difference in what is offered to adults. Soaps are filled with rough, tough male characters, and those who do not fit the mould are seen as wimps or derided as new men. There have been inroads in the last decade – men can be seen to cry on TV – but they haven't gone far enough and hardly challenge the dominant images of men that are presented.

Men who are in the public eye tend to be men who are successful in the world of work. If a family man gets in the news it is more likely to be as a result of abusive or violent behaviour against a partner or child, thus reinforcing the idea that women are the natural carers and men are, if anything, a possible danger to women and children. In this climate, fathers can be anxious about giving their children the close physical contact they need. They may be worried that their children may talk about baths together or hugs and touching in ways that may be interpreted as sexually or physically abusive.

Despite the fact that children's books no longer offer a 'Janet and John' image of the world, in which Janet's mother stays home and does the cooking and cleaning and John's father goes out to work, the power of the written word is overshadowed by the moving images of television. Even the actions of parents seem to pale into insignificance against the all-pervasive power of television and the wider media – the public role model dominates the private one. We met Peter in an earlier chapter who always did the ironing at home, yet his young daughter still said 'Mummy does the ironing' (see page 18).

Parents may feel that they are powerless to influence their sons' behaviour when what they do at home is almost invisible when pitted against the power of the public images. How do these images affect boys?

• Boys act out these gender stereotypes in their play, in an attempt both to understand them and to practise what they see as their future gender roles.
• Boys are still likely to be playing on the floor with construction toys, and girls to be dressing up in the home corner, in most playgroups and nursery schools.
• Most school playgrounds are dominated by the vigorous activities of the boys while the girls are left playing around in the spaces at the edge.

Despite the fact that many of the adults (male and female) who surround children act contrary to these gender stereotypes, they still seem to dominate children's play.

HELPING YOUR SONS BREAK OUT OF THE STEREOTYPES

Parents can do a number of different things to help their sons (and daughters) break out of stereotypical gender behaviour. However, parents do need to have a realistic image of what is possible. Boys, particularly in the public sphere, often feel that they have to present a certain image of themselves. Thus, they may feel able to let their guard down and show non-stereotypical aspects of themselves only in the home and when they are 'out of view'.

BEING A ROLE MODEL OF POSITIVE BEHAVIOUR

It's what you do rather than what you say that speaks loudest to children. It's no good encouraging children to break out of gender roles if such roles determine your actions.

Although the signs parents receive from their children may suggest that they are *not* influenced by parents' actions when it comes to gender roles, this is to a great extent due to the fact that they do not want to be seen as different from their peers. Instead, they want to fit in and be seen to fit in.

'Before we had children I thought to myself, We're going to do it differently from other parents; we aren't going to make

the same mistakes. I was clear that my daughter was not going to be limited by anybody's gender expectations and my son wasn't going to be a macho male.

'Eleven years on I see Kirsty and Jimmy doing all the stereotypical girls' and boys' things. I don't know whether it's because they are programmed to each do their own thing, or because of the pressure on children to act like boys and girls. But it certainly appears as if we parents don't have any influence.' Sarah

However it may appear, parents do have a huge influence on their children in this area, but it is as if the gender options they receive from their parents lie dormant and only come to fruition when peer pressure slackens. Thus, it may not be until early adulthood or even later that parents may see the results of the behaviour that they modelled for their children when they were young.

Parental modelling leaves children with a range of options that they internalise within them as to how to behave as men and women. They take in the models of gender that their parents provide through their childhood, and these become a natural part of their repertoire in adulthood. If and when they become parents themselves, they are likely to be able to offer similar models to their children.

'My mother was the typical little woman who stayed home to look after my father and bring up the children. But in the flush of the women's movement in the 1960s, I decided that I wanted something different for myself and my children.

'It was a struggle for me to be this new kind of woman,

but now, when I look at my grown-up children, I can see how differently they experience and behave in the world. When they were growing up they were typical of boys and girls, but now they are fully rounded characters. Being open and expressive of his feelings seems to come as naturally to John as it does to Joanna, while being firm and assertive seems to be as natural to Joanna as it does to John. At the time I felt frustrated with their behaviour, which seemed so limited by gender, but now I can see that they were learning a lot below the surface.' Patricia

CHANGING UNUSEFUL PATTERNS OF BEHAVIOUR

Modelling takes place on many different levels. Children are not only affected by who does what in the family but also by the way in which things are done.

You may be able to see quite clearly how you can step out of gender roles in obvious areas like the division of labour – such as who earns the money and who does the housework – but underlying attitudes that you hold about men, women and relationships will affect your children as deeply.

In the following example, Graham thought he was providing his children with a different example of a father from the one he experienced when he was a child. Graham was actively involved in his children's lives and appeared to be a completely different person from the remote father with whom he grew up. Although Graham's relationship with Jan looked very different *on the surface*, at a deeper level he was repeating the pattern of the relationship of his own parents, in which Graham, the father, controlled who did what and Jan, the mother, fitted in.

'My father's word was law in my childhood home. I didn't want things to be like that in our family home, so I was determined to be a different kind of father.

'For the first few years of the children's lives, Jan, my wife, and I shared everything down the middle. I was very proud of the way we organised things, so it came as a real shock when I heard Jan say that she hadn't really wanted things to be organised like that. I realised that although our family looked very different from the family I grew up in, I had in fact perpetuated my father's role in determining who would do what.

'I am now struggling to learn to negotiate and compromise – but it is not easy. And I see my son pushing and pushing for what he wants, while my daughter gives in to avoid conflict. I hope that as I change they will learn new ways too.' Graham

Such patterns of behaviour are harder to change than, for example, deciding to be more involved with the children or not to sacrifice yourself for the sake of the children. This is because these patterns are subconscious, and parents may not be aware or may not want to admit to themselves that they are behaving in these ways. Becoming aware of such patterns of behaviour, however difficult it may be to acknowledge them, is the first step towards being able to change them.

Here is another example.

'In my father's eyes it was my brother who was the favourite. I didn't take it so badly because my mother compensated by treating me as if I were special.

'I'm now bringing up Ben and Sarah on my own, and I'm making an effort to make them both feel special and not to favour one over the other. But it's hard to do it. There's a part of me that feels that Sarah is more special, rather as my mother felt towards me, and there's another part of me that has negative feelings towards Ben, perhaps from the bit of me that resented my brother for being my father's favourite.

'I suppose I ought to talk with them to find out how they feel, but I don't quite dare to because it's too close to the bone. I try to treat them the same, and I make a point of telling them each that they are special in their own way. But I can still feel these old feelings bubbling away below the surface.'
Rachael

Rachael is conscious of the favouritism that ran through her childhood and, as a result, consciously struggles to deal differently with her children. However, it requires constant vigilance on her part to ensure that the 'old' patterns of behaviour do not intrude on her relationship with her children. Rachael's biggest fear is to hear that her children feel that favouritism has crept into her relationship, so she avoids the issue in order not to hear what she fears most. Hopefully, Rachael will reach a point where she will be able to relax enough to create space for her children to talk about issues of favouritism in her family, because she no longer feels so hurt by the favouritism from her family of origin. Her role will then be to acknowledge any feelings that her children have of being favoured, or second best, without retreating into defensiveness; she may also wish to share her childhood experiences with them and to try to relate to the children differently in some ways. Children need to be able to talk out their feelings about these issues and to be listened to with as open a heart as parents can manage.

Chapter Six

THE FUTURE

HOW BOYS BECOME MEN

Parental influences on boys can play a significant role in determining the kind of men they turn out to be. A boy's main male role model, his father, and the image that his mother gives him of his father, crucially affect who he becomes. How his mother feels about bringing up a male child, whether she can enjoy his 'boisterous' behaviour and how she manages his differentness from her are important. Whether his father is actively involved in his upbringing, or whether his father, for whatever reason, does not have time for him will influence his sense of himself.

Whether he turns out to be the strong, silent type who rarely shares his inner feelings or the 'emotionally literate' man who is sensitive to his own and others' needs will be greatly affected by what he sees, hears and experiences around him as he grows up. As a boy, he may be able to give only a narrow image of the kind of person he is, but as peer pressure recedes and he approaches young adulthood he will be more able to show his real self.

How his parents interact with him will be significant for him and will affect his future life. If his parents treat him with warmth and affection, then that will predispose him to become a warm and affectionate man. How they talk with and relate to him will shape the way he talks to and relates to others, including his own children if he decides to start a family. And how his parents relate to each other will be a major influence on his relationships with others in general and with a future partner in particular.

Other significant adults in his life, whether they be family, friends or teachers, also play their part in affecting who he turns out to be. At a certain point he is likely to gravitate to men outside the family as role models for him; this may be more marked if he is growing up separated from his father. The importance of such mentors cannot be underestimated, especially as he reaches adolescence and looks to other youngsters and adults for a reflection of who he is. And these others, too, will play a significant role in determining the kind of person he will be.

This all takes place within the context of the wider society that is beamed most powerfully into the home through the television. The media's powerful images are likely to exert a strong control over his outward behaviour right through his childhood, but in adulthood he is likely to show his true character, if it is different.

It is not parents alone who determine the outcome of their children, but parents are a cog, possibly the key cog, in a system that prepares boys (and girls) for the future.

WHAT KIND OF WORLD AWAITS THEM?

The world is changing faster and faster. It's hard to know what world awaits boys as they grow into adulthood. Certainly, on current trends there will be fewer 'traditionally male' jobs and more 'female' jobs. Employment is unlikely to play the key role in forming men's identities that it did in the past. And government may play its part, introducing policies such as paternity leave and paid parental leave (equally available to men and women) to encourage men in their role as carers.

As women play a greater role in the job market, the possibility opens up for men to play a greater role at home. The much-derided 'new man' of the 1990s, who is active both in the world of work and at home, could become a norm for men in the next millennium. But for this to happen, men would need to think of themselves in a new light, and women would need to be prepared to create more space for men to be involved in the home, both with their children and with domestic tasks.

It would not be useful to replace the old stereotype of the uninvolved father with a new one of the involved father. That would be imposing a way of being on men (and women) rather than allowing them to choose how they want to be together. It would be much better for men, women and children if men chose voluntarily to spend more time caring for their children, rather than being with them because they are obliged to – and resenting it – and if women chose to make space for men to be more involved in childcare without feeling that they were being pushed out. But such changes cannot be forced and are likely to take time as men and women learn to negotiate new roles together.

The future is uncertain, but if boys can be brought

up with a flexible sense of who they are – broader than the narrow stereotypes they are now offered – then they will be much more able to respond to the uncertain world in which they find themselves.

INDEX

Resources

READING LIST

Biddulph, Steve: *Manhood: A book about setting men free* (Hawthorn Press, 1998)
A book about what it means to be male and what men need in a changing world

Biddulph, Steve: *Raising Boys* (Thorsons, 1998)
A book for parents bringing up boys, acknowledging the biological differences between boys and girls

Burgess, Adrienne: *Fatherhood Reclaimed: The making of the modern father* (Vermilion, 1997)
This book discusses the role of fathers in bringing up their children

Corneau, Guy: *Absent Fathers, Lost Sons: The search for masculine identity* (Shambhala, 1991)
The impact of father 'absence' on sons and how to overcome it

Downes, Peter and Carey Bennett: *Help Your Child Through Secondary School* (Hodder and Stoughton, 1997)
Includes a chapter on helping boys (and girls) learn more effectively

Faber, Adele and Elaine Mazlish: *How to Talk So Kids Will Listen – And listen so kids will talk* (Avon, US, 1980)
A comprehensive, easy-to-read guide to communication skills for parents

Millard, Elaine: *Differently Literate: Boys, girls and the schooling of literacy* (Falmer Press, 1997)
Addresses contemporary concerns for parents and teachers – why boys are falling behind girls in language-based school subjects

Phillips, Angela: *The Trouble with Boys* (Pandora, 1993)
A book about the socialisation of boys which recognises the differences between boys and girls that society is failing to address

West, Peter: *Fathers, Sons and Lovers* (Hawthorn Press, 1996)
How perceptions of manhood have changed over the generations

USEFUL ORGANISATIONS

Gingerbread
England Adviceline: 0171 336 8183
Scotland Adviceline: 0141 353 0953
Northern Ireland Adviceline: 01232 234568
Wales Adviceline: 01792 648728
National organisation for lone parents

Letterbox Library
Unit 2D, Leroy, 436 Essex Road, London N1 3QP
Tel: 0171 226 1633
A bookclub specialising in non-sexist, multicultural books for children

Parentline
Endway House, The Endway, Benfleet, Essex SS7 2AN
Helpline: 01702 559900
Telephone helpline for parents

Parent Network
Room 2, Winchester House, Kennington Park,
11 Cranmer Road, London SW9 1EJ Tel: 0171 735 1214
*Runs courses for parents on communication with their
children, using many of the ideas covered in this book*

Relate
Herbert Gray College, Little Church Street, Rugby,
Warwickshire CV21 3AP Tel: 01788 573 241
National agency for relationship counselling

Stepfamily
3rd Floor, Chapel House, 18 Hatton Place, London
EC1N 8RU Tel: 0171 209 2460
National organisation for people in stepfamilies

Tamarind Ltd
PO Box 296, Camberley, Surrey GU15 4WD
Tel: 01276 683 979
*For children's books with positive, non-sexist images of
black parents and children*

Working With Men
320 Commercial Way, London SE15 1QN
Tel: 0171 732 9409
*WWM's work includes boys and literacy and they produce
materials for schools on fatherhood*

Young Book Trust
Book House, 45 East Hill, London SW18 2QZ
Tel: 0181 516 2984
Contact the Trust for suggestions of appropriate reading material for your son